PARMENIDES, COSMOS, AND BEING

A PHILOSOPHICAL INTERPRETATION

PANAGIOTIS THANASSAS

PARMENIDES, COSMOS, AND BEING

A PHILOSOPHICAL INTERPRETATION

MARQUETTE
UNIVERSITY
PRESS

Marquette Studies in Philosophy
No. 57
Andrew Tallon, Series Editor

LIBRARY OF CONGRESS CATALOGING-IN-PUBLICATION DATA

Thanassas, Panagiotis, 1967-
  Parmenides, cosmos, and being : a philosophical interpretation / Panagiotis Thanassas.
    p. cm. — (Marquette studies in philosophy ; No. 57)
  Includes bibliographical references (p.   ) and index.
  ISBN-13: 978-0-87462-755-8 (pbk. : alk. paper)
  ISBN-10: 0-87462-755-9 (pbk. : alk. paper)
  1. Parmenides. Nature. 2. Philosophy. I. Parmenides. Nature. English. II. Title.
B235.P23N3837 2007
182'.3—dc22
                                                              2007045180

Cover art: Gorgon, after *Greek Art. Ancient Sculpture* (ed. N. Gialouris). Athens: Ekdotiki Athinon 1994, p. 75.

Association of American University Presses

MARQUETTE UNIVERSITY PRESS
MILWAUKEE

The Association of Jesuit University Presses

CONTENTS

ACKNOWLEDGMENTS

This small book has a rather long history behind it. A first draft emerged in 1997-98 in Munich, where I spent a year as a post-doctoral researcher on a scholarship from the *Deutsche For-schungsgemeinschaft*. I would like to thank Prof. Dieter Bremer (who supervised that project) and Prof. Georg Rechenauer for their comments, criticism and suggestions at that time. My first encounter with Parmenides took place even earlier, in the course of my doctoral dissertation at the University of Tübingen (Thanassas 1997). I feel the deepest gratitude for the supervisor of that thesis, Prof. Rüdiger Bubner, who, even from afar, always took an interest in the course of my philosophical studies since then, until his lamented death in February 2007. I enjoyed many stimulating conversations on Parmenides with Prof. Manchester at Stony Brook University in 1995 and numerous exchanges on the subject since then. Michael Mc-Gettigan took upon himself the difficult task of translating the text into English with the help of Dr. Adrian Switzer, while Kenneth Knies and Dionysis Goutsos contributed valuable comments and proposals. The final amendments were made in Heidelberg, during a sabbatical leave with a scholarship funded by the *Alexander von Humboldt Foundation*.

Heidelberg, April 2007

To the memory of Rüdiger Bubner (1941-2007),
in gratitude.

I

THE POEM AND ITS LEGACY

"So I'm afraid that we'll fail to understand what he said and that we'll fall even far shorter of what he had in mind when he said it": these words of Socrates in Plato's *Theaetetus* (184a) testify to the enormous difficulties Parmenides' poem has caused its interpreters. The same dialogue (183e) describes the poet of Elea with verses from Homer as "venerable and awesome" and as possessing "some altogether grand and noble depth" – a reference that illustrates both the rapid appropriation of his poem by 5th century philosophy, as well as its far-reaching effect.

Considering the profound impression he made on his time, the very paucity of credible sources about his life and activities is remarkable.[1] Tradition gives us little reason to doubt that he composed but a single poem.[2] More controversial is the question of whether the poem's title, *Peri Physeôs* (*On Nature*), was given by the author himself, or appended by later editors.[3] Philosophically more interesting, however, is the biographical

---

1 Some material, mostly anecdotal, can be found in Diogenes Laertius IX.21-3 (= DK28 A1); see also the *Suda*-article on Parmenides. – We use the abbreviation DK for references to the standard sixth edition of Hermann Diels / Walther Kranz: *Die Fragmente der Vorsokratiker* [6]1951 (with various reprints since then). This edition's section A contains indirect testimonies about each Pre-Socratic philosopher and their teachings while section B contains fragments of their writings. Avoiding pedantry, we make references to the fragments of Parmenides by giving only the number of the fragment and the line (e.g. 1.32 or 8.7) and omitting the repetition of "DK28 B."

2 This is explicitly confirmed by Diogenes (cf. DK28 A13).

3 See Simplicius *In De Caelo* 556.25 (= DK28 A14).

problem of accurately dating Parmenides' life, since it bears on his relation to Heraclitus. While ancient biographers place his *acmê* at approximately 500 B.C.,[4] he appears in Plato's *Parmenides* (127b-c) as a 65 year old man conversing with a "still very young" Socrates. This meeting would have to have taken place around 450 B.C.; Parmenides' birth date would have been 515 and he therefore could have easily been acquainted with Heraclitus' writing. Still, an interpretive sensitivity to the literary character of Plato's dialogues, to his dramaturgy and his "staging" techniques, suggests that Plato here presents a meeting that could not possibly have taken place.[5] The far more credible reconstruction of the Presocratic history of philosophy presented in the *Sophistes* (242d) has the "Ionian muses," i.e. Heraclitus, *follow* the "Eleatic people." Accordingly, Parmenides must have written his poem, notably composed in an archaic style, around or before 500 B.C., i.e. before Heraclitus' highly elaborate statements.[6]

Parmenides' choice of poetic form and the epic hexameter in particular distinguishes his work from Ionian prose and links him to the tradition of Homer and (especially) Hesiod. The surviving fragments of the poem amount to a total of 154 verses, most of them complete. The first 32 verses contain the

---

4 Cf. DK28 A1.

5 Among else, because of the punctilious reminders of the interlocutors' age, which is virtually unique in the Platonic corpus. Thus, when Guthrie writes that "Plato [...] had no reason to give such exact information about their ages unless he knew it to be correct" (1965: 2), the reverse is actually the case: Plato would have had no reason to provide such trivial details unless he wanted to present as credible something that in reality could not have taken place. See also Allen (1983: 64).

6 See a similar argument provided by Reinhardt (1916: 60-4, 215-22, and passim). For further support of the dating proposed here, see Diels (1897: 71) and Hölscher (1968: 161). For recent argumentation in favor of the opposite view, see Graham (2002).

proemium, which describes a wondrous chariot ride. Accompanied by Sun-maidens and carried by steeds, the poet is led through the "gates of the paths of Night and Day," the location of which remains unspecified. Past the gates he encounters a goddess who welcomes him in a friendly manner.

The rest of the poem is presented as a speech of this goddess, who remains anonymous throughout. She promises to grant Parmenides insight into the "truth" (*alêtheia*) as well as into human "opinions" (*doxai*). In accordance with this programmatic statement, the poem is divided into a section on Aletheia, which concentrates on "Being," and a section on Doxa, which treats of the Cosmos and its phenomena. Aletheia is taken up by 78, while Doxa by 44 of the surviving verses, though this proportion in no way corresponds to the proportions within the original poem. Doxa was originally much longer than Aletheia, and Diels was probably correct in his estimation that we possess "9/10 of the Aletheia [...] and, according to a less certain appraisal, perhaps 1/10 of the Doxa."[7]

The Aletheia section begins (fr. 2) with the depiction of the "only" two routes that are possible "for thinking." The one ("that Is and that it is impossible not-to-be") is the path of Being, the other ("that Is-not and that it is necessary not-to-be") is the path of Non-Being. The structure of the entire Aletheia is determined by the opposition between these two routes, affirming the first and rejecting the second. The route of Being is that of "persuasion," since it "follows upon truth"; the route of Non-Being, however, remains "without any tidings," since Non-Being can "neither be known nor expressed." Thought and Being are then said to be "the same" (fr. 3), the essential property of Thinking lying in its ability to "see" absent things as present (fr. 4). As for the "mortals' opinions," which will

---

7   Diels (1897: 25-6). – I write Aletheia and Doxa in capital letters and in the singular when I refer to the first and the second part of the poem respectively, without any presumptions concerning the content or the epistemic status of these parts.

be the subject of the second part, they are already subjected to a remorseless critique in the Aletheia (frs. 6, 7): The "two-headed" mortals repeatedly wander down a third quasi-path by overlooking the unbridgeable contradiction between the two ontological routes. This oversight occasions a blind confusion of the paths and unwittingly commits mortals to Non-Being.

The eighth fragment announces the famous "signs" of Being (8.1-4) and presents them in detail: The "Being" (*eon*) introduced here is shown to be [a] "ungenerated and imperishable" (8.5-21), [b] "whole and unique" (8.22-5), [c] "unmovable" and "unshaken" (8.26-31), and finally [d] "complete" (8.32-3 and 42-9). All signs have in common that they result from the continual demand to negate Non-Being in order to combat its presence both in the pre-philosophical world-view and in the traditional cosmologies. This *eon* is "ungenerated" because, from an ontological perspective, what is generated can only have arisen from Nothing. It is "whole and unique" because only Non-Being would differ from it, and precisely Non-Being is to be rejected. It is "unmovable" and "unshaken" because motion could only take place in something external to and other than it – but here again there can be nothing external to Being. *Eon*'s "completeness," finally, is an outcome of the conclusions just reached, and is illustrated by the image of the "well-rounded sphere." Just as all positions on the surface of the sphere are "equally strong everywhere from the centre," so are all existing things equal to one another and interconnected as beings – because of the absence of Non-Being.

The goddess concludes her "convincing account and thought about truth" and proceeds to "mortal opinions" (8.50-1) that are traced back to the "establishing" and "naming" of two forms: Light and Night. These function as the basic principles throughout the Doxa, principles that explain not only human perception of the world, but also the real world itself. The goddess describes her speech at first as "deceitful" (8.52) and begins to discuss a human error (8.54), whereupon she promises

(8.60) to present the entire "appearing world-arrangement" (*eoikôs diakosmos*) in an "appropriate" manner (this is a further meaning of *eoikôs*). Fr. 10 illustrates her plan: she will present the "generation" (*physis*) and the "works" (*erga*) of the aether, sun, moon and heaven, thus treating the cosmogonic question of the origin as well as the cosmological question of the current state of the entire world as it appears. She will do so, she says, (8.61) in an unsurpassable manner.

Little remains of the detailed realization of this project, and even the indirect tradition has devoted only sparse, often contradictory reports to this part of the poem. Nothing seems certain except that all worldly processes are interpreted as mixtures of the basic forms of Light and Night, and of their "signs" or "powers" (9); the same holds for the epistemological interpretation of human "thought" (16). And while the temporal threefold "was – is – will be" was deemed irrelevant to ontological inquiry in the Aletheia (8.5), in what appears to have been the concluding fragment (19) the cosmic process is described in just such temporal terms: "In this way, according to the opinion, these things were born and now are, and hereafter, having grown up, they will reach their end."

Parmenides quickly became a philosophical authority, but from early on his work was viewed with a measure of embarrassment and helplessness. In due course the opinion had become widespread that the actual sense of his statements could no longer be reconstructed. Although single verses from his poem were selected as late as the 6th century of the Common Era to add weight to a variety of positions and assertions, his fundamental philosophical concerns remained somewhat inscrutable, and copies of the poem became increasingly rare. It is primarily to the Neo-Platonist Simplicius that we owe the rescue of extensive fragments from the poem. Because of the "rarity of the text" (DK28 A21), Simplicius decided to include long passages from it in his commentary on Aristotle's *Physics*. Further fragments have come down to us from Theophrastus, Plutarch, Sextus Empiricus, Clemens, Plotinus, and Proclus.[8]

As we have said, the encounter between the aging Parmenides and the young Socrates as portrayed in the dialogue *Parmenides* recounts an imaginary event and must be considered a product of Plato's literary art. Not even the content of the dialogue, whose arguments are largely conducted in the vocabulary of a Platonic theory of Forms, provides reliable information about the authentic Parmenidean philosophy. It would, however, be difficult to overestimate the effect of a Socratic remark directed to Parmenides in this dialogue: "you say in the poem that everything is one" (*hen to pan*, 128a-b). This synopsis of Parmenides' philosophy in the formula "everything is one," which also appears in other passages of the Corpus Platonicum,[9] together with the interpretation of the philosophy of Being as a crude and austere monistic doctrine, will henceforth dominate the entire history of Parmenides interpretation from Plato to the present. The concept of Being, which was in fact the only authoritative and relevant concept for Parmenides, is suppressed in favor of a "One" that radically calls into question cosmic plurality, multiplicity and motion, and speaks against the reality of appearances.

Aristotle reinforces this interpretation when he counts Parmenides among those "unphysical" philosophers[10] who "annulled generation and destruction altogether" from the world. Nonetheless, he does accept that Parmenides' philosophy of Being refers to sensible entities (*aisthêtas ousias*) and has nothing else as its object:[11] Parmenides and the Eleatics do "refer to

---

8 For further details, see especially Coxon (1986: 1-7).

9 Cf. among others *Soph.* 242d, 244b, *Theait.* 180e.

10 See Sextus, *Adv. math.* X, 46 (= DK28 A26).

11 *De Caelo* 298b 14, 20 (= DK28 A25).

physis, but they do not articulate physical aporiae."[12] According to Aristotle, Parmenides' error consists in the fact that, although his philosophy addressed nothing but the world in its entirety, he committed himself to an "unphysical" ontology, which was incapable of investigating the state and constitution of the world as such. From the perspective of his own doctrine of categories, Aristotle asserted that "Being" and "One" "are said in numerous ways" (*pollachôs legesthai*) and that such polysemy makes Parmenidean monism of "the one Being" untenable.[13] Thus, in contrast to Plato, Aristotle did not ignore the second part of Parmenides' poem, the so-called Doxa; but he obviously remained helpless in the face of its account of the world of appearance in a cosmogonic and cosmological system based on the principles of "Light and Night." Aristotle recognized in the Doxa a certain retreat from rigid monism, and he imputed to Parmenides the belief that "there is one according to *logos*, but there are many according to perception." This concession to plurality, however, is interpreted by Aristotle as a grudging result of Parmenides' being "compelled to follow the phenomena."[14] The question of the relationship between the truth of Being and the world of appearance remains thereby unasked.

As expected, reference to the Doxa was also made by those few ancient authors who refused to understand Parmenides as denying the reality of the world. The most prominent example was Plutarch's defense of Parmenides against the attacks of the Epicurean Colotes.[15] A further, though philosophically less significant, defense is found in Simplicius' underscoring

---

12 This is, in my view, the correct reading of a passage from *Physics* 185a 18-9; see on this also Mansion (1945: 66).

13 See *Physics* A2, esp. 185a 20 ff.

14 *Met.* 986b 31 ff.

15 See *Adv. Colotem* 1113e-1114e (partly reproduced as DK28 A34).

of Parmenides' common sense: "obviously Parmenides was not ignorant of the fact that he had been born himself and that he had two feet, when he described Being as one."[16]

Despite all this, Parmenides was again and again accused of denying the reality of the phenomenal world. Decisive in this respect was not so much Plato's own dictum that "all is one," but rather the overpowering force of Platonism and its "two-world-doctrine" that assumes the separate existence of an "intelligible" and a "sensible" world and regards Forms as transcendent substances. It was to this distorted, ultimately anti-Platonic image of Plato that Parmenides' philosophy was made to conform, thus elevating it to the prototype of a vulgar world-denying Platonism. While in Plato's thought the "sensible world" still maintains its status, if only as ontologically deficient, in the "Platonized" Parmenides it disappears altogether, dismissed as deception and illusion. Illuminating in this regard is the interpretation of the chariot ride in the poem's proemium as an "ascent" that anticipates the climb into the Beyond portrayed in Plato's *Phaedrus*. But this proemium does not contain the least reference to an upward "ascent"; instead, it leaves the topography of the chariot's path strikingly vague, describing the ride only as a departure from the usual, customary and normal. Not surprisingly, the highpoint of this Platonizing interpretation of Parmenides is found in Neo-Platonism, in which Parmenidean Being is utterly reinterpreted as a prelude to the Neo-Platonic One.

Even today, the notion of *monism* determines research on Parmenides to a great extent. It is too seldom acknowledged that even a statement such as "all is one" cannot eliminate plurality, but rather implies a dialectical relationship between unity and multiplicity and in no way permits an adaptation into an assertion of the type "there is only one thing whose name

---

16 *In De Caelo* 559.

is Being."[17] Yet most interpretations tend to make just such an assumption, however they may go on to interpret or evaluate it. The direct path to this view is taken in the interpretation of the Parmenidean *eon* as a collective noun referring to the totality of all that is – a totality which is thus melted down to an undifferentiated unity, giving rise to that peculiar unworldly creature called "the one Being."

Despite this unattractive portrayal of Parmenides, research into his philosophy has steadily increased over the last several decades. Heidegger's turn to the Pre-Socratics and his own philosophy of Being have certainly contributed to a greater interest in Parmenides. But even more important was the progressive differentiation of perspectives from which Parmenides could be viewed and interpreted, combined with a corresponding liberality of the hermeneutic approaches. Even though interpreters seldom question Parmenidean "monism," they no longer take aim at it and its puzzling consequences; instead they prefer to reconstruct the train of thought that may have led Parmenides to such conclusions.

One of the most important impulses in the research of the last century has doubtless been given by *analytic philosophy*. Under its inspiration, propositional logic has been used to interpret the two routes of "Being" and "Non-Being" as general forms of positive and negative predication. First recommended by Calogero (1932), the "logical-verbal" origin of Parmenides' philosophy has gained canonical status in Anglo-American research.[18] This approach, which is occasionally instructive, ulti-

---

17 A culmination of this naivety ascribed to Parmenides, which in fact reveals only the naivety of his interpreters, can be found in the following rather astonishing remark of Popper: "the world consists, in reality, of one huge, unmoving, homogenous, solid block of spherical shape in which nothing can ever happen" (1998: 79-80). – Against this "numerical monism," P. Curd (1998) has recently opted for a "predicational monism" (see below, pp. 32-3, n. 10).

18 See Mourelatos (1979).

mately remains unconvincing, and this for several reasons. First of all, the equation of the propositional form of negation with the Non-Being rejected by Parmenides fails to explain why Parmenides himself continues to use negation throughout the poem. Secondly, it is anachronistic to make Parmenides a participant in the "linguistic turn" *avant la lettre* and to interpret his weighty ontological assertions as mere reflections on linguistic usage. Finally, it is even more dubious to think that such linguistic reflection could lay the foundation for "monism," thus effectively elevating language to a criterion of reality.

Another group of interpreters saw in Parmenides' introduction of the routes of Being and Non-Being the first attestation of *formal logic's* elementary principles (e.g. the "principle of non-contradiction"[19] or the "principle of the excluded middle"[20]), while others saw in Parmenides' decision for Being an application of these principles and the outcome of a formal proof, e.g. in the way of "a disjunctive syllogism, the so-called *modus tollendo ponens.*"[21] Such attempts, however, are always on the lookout for a formal logic that only became necessary after the Sophistic adventure and received its first formulation by Aristotle. Forcing Parmenides' thought into syllogistic schemata is not destined for success, which is why most such attempts either assume the existence of missing verses or, more frequently, confine themselves to bringing to light certain "fallacies" committed by Parmenides and to reproaching him for such "errors."

These and similar efforts take only the first half of the poem into consideration and usually consign to oblivion the section

---

19 Reinhardt (1916: 30); see also transl. in Mourelatos (1974: 296).

20 Heitsch (1974: 87, 116).

21 Thus Mansfeld (1964: 58). Verdenius (1942: 41) also tries to reconstruct the Parmenidean argument by means of three syllogisms, while Barnes (1982: 165-7) even discovers some 17 argumentative steps.

on Doxa and its turn to the world of phenomena. Neglect of this section, however, can no longer be explained away as an oversight. In 1916, Karl Reinhardt fundamentally transformed the landscape of Parmenides research precisely by means of his explicit inquiry into the relation between Aletheia and Doxa. Before Reinhardt's work, Doxa was considered a "presentation of opinions held by others," or else it was accorded a "merely hypothetical significance." Both of these perspectives, first adumbrated by Zeller,[22] were then adopted by Diels and Wilamowitz and further developed into the *doxographic-eristic* and the *hypothetical* interpretation of the Doxa section. Thus, according to Diels, the Doxa serves only the "propaedeutic purposes of the [Eleatic] School."[23] This lets Parmenides appear as the first historian of philosophy, who wanted to offer his students a compendium of opinions held by others in order to familiarize them with the doctrines of opposing Schools. According to Wilamowitz, by contrast, the second part of the poem offers a "self-sufficient and consistent hypothesis alongside the truth."[24]

Both views have been subjected to a withering critique by Reinhardt. Against Diels, he drew attention both to the complete absence of any polemics against other philosophers and to the originality of the Doxa section.[25] Against Wilamowitz, he pointed out the entirely un-"hypothetical" and utterly "apodictic" tone of the Doxa, as well as the "absurdity" of assuming a "consistent hypothesis" that rests "on a principle opposite to truth."[26]

---

22 Zeller ([2]1856: 418; [6]1919: 725).

23 Diels (1897: 63).

24 Wilamowitz (1899: 204-5).

25 Reinhardt (1916: 26-8). It is significant that Philoponus already had to contend with a doxographic interpretation; see *In Phys.* 21.30.

26 Reinhardt (1916: 25-6). Schwabl also stresses that what we encounter in the Doxa is an "almost dogmatic doctrine" (1968: 400).

After Reinhardt's powerful attacks against the "eristic" and the "hypothetical" approach exposed the difficulties involved in an interpretation of the Doxa, he himself undertook the task of giving a convincing account of the relation between the two parts of the poem. Here, he was guided by the principle that "the part can be understood only out of the whole, cosmogony only out of ontology."[27] The conflict between the two sides of this methodological guideline is evident. While its first half reaffirms an old hermeneutic rule, the second half makes one part of the poem dependent on the other. In this shift are contained the overall limitations in Reinhardt's resolution. The second part of the poem, which, it must be remembered, was considerably longer than the Aletheia, becomes in his interpretation a mere appendix, or at best a subordinate domain, in which "truth" is, as it were, subsequently applied. Wielding his newly discovered "weapon of logic," Parmenides would here "derive" the world itself from the "logical" laws and "basic forms" of the first part of the poem.[28] In a manner parallel to the scholars he criticized (Diels and Wilamowitz), Reinhardt ultimately remained imprisoned by the conception of Doxa as "illusion," overlooking those central fragments of the poem (like 10 or 11) which promise some insight into the nature of the –altogether real– world of phenomena.

Apart from the inadequacy of his own solution of a "purely logical"[29] relation between Aletheia and Doxa, and apart from the unconvincing supposition of a "more logical than physical origin"[30] of the cosmogony, Reinhardt created a standard still worthy of respect by Parmenides researchers in the century following his own. The question of the relation between the

27 Reinhardt (1916: 17).

28 Reinhardt (1916: 74-82); see also transl. in Mourelatos (1974: 305-11).

29 Reinhardt (1916: 79); transl. in Mourelatos (1974: 308).

30 Reinhardt (1916: 71); transl. in Mourelatos (1974: 305).

two parts of the poem and the demand for "mediation" of one kind or another still remain the Lydian stone of any meaningful interpretation. Empty phrases still in circulation, presenting Doxa as the "propagation of untruths"[31] and the world as an "unreal show" or a sort of "hallucination or dream,"[32] as well as descriptions of the Doxa as "untenable" or simply as "false,"[33] should no longer play a role in Parmenides studies. Likewise, approaches to the Doxa that attempt to rehabilitate the old eristic-doxographic reading, and thus see it as a "second-hand"[34] narrative, are now rare exceptions. It is now almost univocally recognized that the second part does not contain a "characterizing of colleagues,"[35] just as it cannot be merely an "inventory list of some erroneous opinions."[36] At the same time, the significance ascribed to the Doxa by Reinhardt also points the way toward liberating Parmenides from the ballast of "Platonizing" and Neo-Platonic interpretations that have been imposed on the poem. The inclusion of the Doxa section and the (utterly real) world presented there in an interpretation of the whole makes clear that this poem can never have been a treatise "On the One."

---

31 According to Barnes (1982: 156).

32 Guthrie (1965: 65, 75).

33 So Mansfeld (1964: 122, 210) or Gallop (1984: 21), recently again Sedley (1999: 123).

34 According to Owen (1960: 88).

35 Gadamer (GW 7: 58).

36 Held (1980: 547).

2

THE HEART OF TRUTH

After the goddess kindly welcomes the poet and praises his good fortune, she promises (1.28) to let him "learn everything." This totality at which she takes aim includes the whole of knowledge and takes two different forms. On the one hand, the adept will see through to the "unshaken heart of persuasive truth" (1.29), the inner kernel that grounds and justifies all other particular truths. On the other hand, he will understand the "mortals' opinions, in which there is no true conviction" (1.30). This first sweeping and vague dismissal of the "opinions" becomes more concrete in the next verse: "But nevertheless," adds the goddess, using two adversatives (*all' empês*), "these you shall learn as well" – whereupon follow the two final verses of the proemium (1.31-2), which remain the poem's most controversial lines. The only certainty in these verses seems to be the fact that, while the subjective opinions themselves (*doxai*) lack conviction, their objects, the appearing things (*dokounta*), are granted a certain positivity ("acceptably," *dokimôs*) to. But how far does this positivity extend?

The traditional reading of these verses states that "appearing things [...] should pervade (*perônta*) everything." This view is actually a relic of an old, now clearly untenable reading.[1] More importantly, the phrase "appearing things pervade everything" can hardly be given a clear sense – for what might be that "everything," which is different from "appearing things" and pervaded by them? In the last few decades, the reading *per*

---

1 Diels (1897: 58) read *perônta* in connection with a verb *dokimôs'[ai]*. This possibility has long been refuted; cf. Reinhardt (1916: 6).

onta has come to be preferred as a clearly superior alternative.[2] Yet this option remains unsatisfactory as long as it yields the meaning: "what appears is everything." Such a complete and utter dominance of appearance would never have been proclaimed "acceptable" by the goddess.[3] We therefore propose to understand the participle *onta* not as a copula but in an "absolutive" syntactic construction, and to attribute to it the entire ontological weight of the verb "to be" that we encounter in other parts of Parmenides' poem: "all that appears *is*."[4] Under

---

2   Especially since Mourelatos set out that the verb *peran* never means "pervade" in the sense of "pass through and then occupy" or "govern," but always "get through and leave behind," "get on the other side of" (1970: 213).

3   This is the reading of Owen (1960: 88), Guthrie (1965: 9), Curd (1998: 113), and many other adherents of *per onta*, who therefore see in the last two lines of the proemium not a transition to ontological truth but a description of erroneous Doxa.

4   More on this point in Thanassas (1997: 36-41). The crucial point in the grammar here is that the participle *onta* holds no predicate; *panta* is not a predicate, but simply replaces *dokounta*. It is only Mourelatos and Owens that seem to have read the expression in this way. Mourelatos, whose contribution to establishing the version *per onta* was decisive, translates: "just being all of them altogether" (1970: 216), or "if only all of them were in every way" (1999: 125); Owens's gloss: "all indeed beings," "all indeed existent" (1974: 385). In the same article on "The Physical World of Parmenides," a masterpiece of Parmenides studies that remains completely neglected, Owens stresses that for Parmenides "all sensible things have being, far more being than the ordinary mentality is willing to concede to any one of them. [...] any denial of the reality of the physical world would do away with the reality of being, and its reduction to an illusionary status would make being likewise an illusion. The one stable being and the multiple and changing perceptible world are the same thing, as known respectively through reasoning and through sensation" (1974: 395).

this interpretation, the complete translation of the verses 1.31-2 would read:

> But nevertheless these you shall learn as well, how appearing things should be accepted: all of them altogether as beings.[5]

The significance of both verses can hardly be overestimated. The adept is here asked to enter into a learning process (*mathêseai*), within which "what appears" (*dokounta*) is not only rescued, as it were, as the object of those previously discredited beliefs (*doxai*), but also becomes the only object and point of reference for the question of Being. The last two lines of the proemium mark the *transition from mortal beliefs to ontological truth*.

This interpretation finds further support in certain observations about the structure of lines 1.28-32. The double emphasis on necessity in lines 28 and 32 (*chreô* or *xrên*) relates in both

5 We thus propose the following grammatical understanding of this controversial passage: a) In contrast to Reinhardt's solution (1916: 9) and to most interpreters after him, we take the verb *chrên* in the sense called elsewhere by Reinhardt himself (1916: 7) the "customary" one: as a "counterfactual" *irrealis*, which asks us to overcome the mortals' prior manner of dealing with appearances and sets out the conditions for accepting these appearances (similarly also Mourelatos 1970: 205-6). b) The reading of *per onta* should not succumb to the worry that Parmenides ought to have employed here the Ionic form *eonta*. We encounter the form *on* not only in the line 8.57 (admittedly corrupt in part), but also in authors such as Xenophanes (DK21 B22.2) or Empedocles (DK31 B129.5). c) The particle *per* has an intensifying function, stressing that *everything* that appears is; *per onta* therefore need not be understood as an adversative, which would perhaps render it untenable. Although *per* in conjunction with the participle *ôn* almost always has an adversative meaning, this is highly unlikely in cases such as *Ilias* 1.352 or *Scutum* 189, whereas in *Ilias* 24.749 the adversative is altogether out of question. But even if one remains dissatisfied with this reading, a return to the definitely refuted *perônta* seems to us no longer possible. In this case, a further conjecture should be sought (i.e. along the lines of *panta g' eonta*).

cases to a specific totality ("learn everything" and "all of them as beings"). In the first case, this totality is epistemological and encompasses both Aletheia and Doxa; in the second case, however, it is an ontological totality that no longer divides into two. As for the words closing each of the verses (*dokounta* and *onta*), they do not refer to different objects, but rather to the one totality of appearances that are acceptable only when grasped "as beings." This possibility of grasping all appearances "as beings" is nothing other than the possibility of ontology. The closing word *onta* thus proves to be the high point of the entire ontological program projected by the goddess, the only goal of the "route of Being" about to be presented.

If the subject matter of Being and its only point of reference is the totality of *dokounta*, then Being is no "transcendent" object at all, no robust unitary structure or substance which puts into question and undermines the multiplicity of the world.[6] It is experienced on the side of phenomena and as belonging to them, belonging to the world of appearance. It supplies a measure for accepting (*dokimôs*) a form of knowledge that is directed toward the world and that is now possible as ontological knowledge. Accordingly, the frequently discussed problem of the relation between Aletheia and Doxa takes on a new significance: Both modes of cognition (and thus both parts of the poem) do not relate to different classes of objects, but rather to the *one* totality of appearances, which are grasped in the Doxa as merely appearing, but in the Aletheia "as beings."

6 In addition to Owens (1974; see p. 24, n. 4 above) and to an article of de Rijk (1983) influenced by him, Finkelberg has also made the claim that "Being is consistent with material heterogeneity" and denotes "a unified notion of the manifold" (1999: 233, 235); but he then seems to deprive Being of its noetic character, when he calls it "spatially extended" and "spherical."

The goddess invites her adept to think two "routes of inquiry": the first affirms the "Is," while the second is pledged to the "Is-not." The fact that Being is discovered on a route (upon which one must steadily move!) and is attained as the outcome of agile searching should undermine any labeling of Parmenides as a prophet of rigidity and immobility.

When Being and Non-Being are first announced, they are not merely stated, but intensified by modal expressions:

"The one [route, to think][7] that Is and that it is impossible not-to-be" (2.3)

"The other [route, to think] that Is-not and that it is necessary not-to-be" (2.5)

The modal complements "impossible not-to-be" and "necessary not-to-be" underscore the unconditional, categorical character of the decision demanded here. The two routes of this ontological crossroads stand in a contradictory relation and form a complete disjunction.[8] By her assurance that there are "only" two routes, the goddess wishes to deny any possible "middle way."[9] The alternative between 2.3 and 2.5 is an exhaustive one. It is precisely the vacillation back and forth between Being and Non-Being (6.8, 8.40) that is here considered the greatest danger for the philosophy of Being, and that motivates the goddess' demand for strict attitudes and unambiguous approaches.

The notion of Being as "not Nothing" and the necessity of an explicit denial of Non-Being are recurring themes throughout

---

7 For the advantages of supplementing "to think" instead of the usual "says," cf. Cordero (2004: 42).

8 The ontological crossroads presented in fr. 2 can be formalized in the following way (where A stands for the affirmation "Is"):

2.3: A and necessarily $\neg\neg$A.

2.5: $\neg$A and necessarily $\neg$A.

9 Owen, however, had such a middle way in view: "the subject *can* but need not exist, [...] the question 'Does it exist?' has to be answered sometimes yes and sometimes no" (1960: 91).

the poem. Thus, the concept of Being does not disintegrate into an undifferentiated "indeterminate immediacy,"[10] but receives its first concrete determination in its opposition to Non-Being. Being and Non-Being, as well as their respective routes, are always mentioned together (6.1-2, 8.11, 8.16). More importantly, the very route of Being introduces (and negates) the opposing Non-Being ("impossible not-to-be"), while the route of Non-Being includes an effort to prove the impossibility of Being.[11] The denial of Non-Being thus emerges as a *constitutive moment of Being itself and of its route*. In the same manner, the route of Non-Being can be determined simply as the ultimate, rigorous and uncompromising negation of Being ("necessary not-to-be"). Parmenides did not "stop at mere Being,"[12] but always took into account the possibility of a conversion into Non-Being, and made the prompt negation of this conversion a crucial requirement of his ontology. That both ontological categories belong together[13] in no way implies that they are of equal status. The requisite decision is always made in favor of Being, and the second route (that of Non-Being) is described as soon as it is introduced as a "path without any tidings." For, as the goddess immediately states, "neither could you know Non-Being –for this is impossible– nor could you express it" (2.7-8).

---

10 See Hegel, ch. "Being" in *The Science of Logic*.

11 This is correctly observed and emphasized by Cordero, who however concludes that "it makes no sense to speak of a 'way of being' as opposed to a 'way of not-being,' since both ways speak of being and not-being" (2004: 72). This criticism overlooks the evident fact that the routes speak of Being and Non-Being in different, in fact antithetical ways.

12 Hegel, *Encyclopaedia*, § 86, Addition.

13 Heidegger in particular has underscored this (1935: 119); see also Thanassas (1997: 78-80).

The triad "Being – Thinking – Saying" delineates the domain of Parmenidean ontology. By the very introduction of the crossroads, Being is declared to be the only concern and subject matter of this ontology. The argumentation in favor of the route of Being in fr. 2 is not carried out according to formal rules of syllogisms (rules that, in any case, were developed much later). This argumentation can therefore neither be reconstructed by means of formal logic, nor measured and evaluated by it. The status of both routes is determined explicitly according to the knowledge that can be obtained along their respective ways, and according to the communicability of this knowledge. In this context, the route of Being does not require a formal-logical corroboration, but is rather demonstrated from the very beginning –and thanks to its overwhelming evidence– to be the "path of persuasion" that "follows upon truth" (2.4). The asseveration of the simple "Is" denotes an ultimate assertion of something that does not depend upon a syllogistic argument, but is legitimated by divine revelation and intended to function itself as the measure of every further argument, reasoning, and "decision" (*krisis*).

On the second route, nothing can be sought, much less discovered. This argument from the unknowability and unutterability of Non-Being is not a formal one, but instead seeks to charge ontology with the duty to aim only at what can be articulated and communicated.[14] The voiceless inner experience of a supposed "unio mystica" with Being[15] is thus disallowed from the very beginning. The soon to be determined deficiency of the second route does not mean, however, that it can simply be forgotten; nor does the unknowability of Non-Being con-

---

14 Similarly Curd, who insists that "there has not been a proof of the unacceptability of the way of not-being" and that the second route is "introduced as impossible" (1998: 33).

15 This was the core of Fränkel's interpretation of the poem (1975: 366).

tradict the original demand to think *both* routes.[16] What is un-knowable (2.7) is Non-Being to be taken as the quasi-content of the second route.[17] The route itself is simply "without any tidings" (2.6), but must always be taken into account, in order that thought may precisely determine its task on the route of Being and keep in mind the incessant danger of going astray.

---

16 Both Mansfeld (1964: 56) and Kahn (1969: 703) saw a contradiction in this.

17 Wiesner (1996: 109) comes to the same conclusion.

3. *ESTI,* BEING AND THINKING

Being is repeatedly named throughout the poem, and in different ways and variations: "Being is" (*eon emmenai* or *esti einai*, 6.1), "that Is" (*hôs estin*, 8.2), "either Is or Is-not" (*estin ê ouk estin*, 8.16). Already in the first announcement of the routes, the remarkable concision of the form "Is" (*estin*) raises the question of how to describe the verb semantically and define it syntactically. It is customary to assign to "Is" either an existential meaning, or a predicative function. Yet, an *existential* "Is" confirms the existence of a certain entity and thus requires supplementation by a subject. This subject can hardly be *eon*,[1] which appears much later in the poem as a conceptual invention, and certainly cannot function here as an implied subject of *estin.* On the other hand, a "formal" subject, like "what can be thought or spoken of,"[2] would, in the final analysis, ascribe to Parmenides something as absurd as the affirmation of the existence of life on Mars.[3] But apart from the interpretive problems that come with the hypothesis of an existential "Is," one might also ask why Parmenides would conceal the subject of the "Is" if he really did intend for there to be one.[4]

---

1 As was attempted by Zeller ([2]1856: 398), Diels (1897: 33), and Reinhardt (1916: 35).

2 Owen (1960: 94-5).

3 Furth (1968: 249) drew this abstruse conclusion. Long, on the contrary, insisted rightly that "it is time to stop supposing that our capacity to 'think of' non-existent objects like unicorns, has any critical bearing on Parmenides" (2005: 234).

4 It was Mourelatos who raised this question and made clear its consequences (1970: 273). If however one still insisted on searching for an

Supporters of a *predicative* "Is," oriented to propositional logic,[5] must on their part accuse Parmenides of confusing the predicative and existential usages. Calogero was the first to interpret "Is" as "the general and universal form" of every affirmative judgment. On his view, this form was subjected by Parmenides to an "ontological hypostatization," while the rejection of the second route made the elimination of all negative predication possible.[6] Raven, on his part, set out from the assumption that Non-Being is unknowable because it is nonexistent, and derived from this existential notion a prohibition against negative predication.[7] But as was noted previously,[8] Parmenides could not have intended or justified such a prohibition.

However, we must not lose sight of the fact that these and similar readings do not mean to say that "Is" in 2.3 is *itself* a copula, but that it is instead an (unsuccessful) Parmenidean reflection *about* the use of the copula. This was expressed with utmost clarity in Mourelatos' *metalinguistic* interpretation of the "Is" as a "bare copula" that aims at "speculative predication": at a "theoretical examination"[9] that yields propositions of the form "– is –" or "x is F," in which F is the "characteristic nature, true identity, intrinsic reality, or essence" of each and every x.[10]

---

implicit subject of *estin*, we would propose only *dokounta*; according to our reading of 1.31-32 (s. above, p. 23-6): *ta dokounta esti*!

5 See above, p. 18-9.

6 Calogero (1932: 6-7, 21).

7 Kirk/Raven (1957: 269-70).

8 See above, p. 18.

9 Mourelatos (1970: 51, 58).

10 Mourelatos (1976: 46, 53). The direction of Curd's "predicational monism" is similar: "each thing that is can be only one thing; it can hold only the one predicate that indicates what it is, and must hold it in a particularly strong way" (1998: 66). For some interesting reservations raised by him against this parallel interpretation, see

Parmenides need no longer stand accused of logical confusions
and absurd consequences; in particular, it is no longer tenable
to assume that he established a prohibition against negative
statements. Instead, we can see the ontological crossroads as
a warning against the significance of negative statements for
cosmology, but also against the possibility of a "constitutive
negation [...] *in* the world."[11] The immense merit of Mourelatos was to show the significance of the theme of the "route"
and the notion of "seeking" or "inquiry" (*dizêsis*) on the route
of Being. This achievement does not compel us, however, to
view Parmenides as a "meta-cosmologist,"[12] as a philosopher
of science and a methodologist *avant la lettre*, who assigns his
"Is" merely the role of a "conveyer."[13] We would rather insist
that *estin* is always completed in itself and requires no further
specifications or assignments.

Mourelatos (1999). The valuable merit of Curd's much-acclaimed
interpretation is that it frees Parmenides from the obtuse monism
usually ascribed to him (see p. 16-8 above) and rehabilitates plural-
ism as compatible with the theoretical enterprise of Parmenides: "it is
possible for there to be a numerical plurality of entities each of which
is predicationally one" (1998: 5). Cordero's notion of a "linguistic"
monism (2004: 176) also points in a similar direction, although he
seems to disregard that the "oneness detectable in Parmenides" is
not "only [...] linguistic," but also noetic. In an interesting essay,
Rapp explores a further possibility of "predicational monism" that
goes beyond Curd's "essentialism" (2005: 303): "it is the word 'to be'
itself and only this word that [...] can exclusively be predicated of
everything that is" (2005: 292). We see this rendering as parallel to
our own interpretation, stressing however that this exclusivity holds
only for the Aletheia and the ontology expounded there. Within this
ontology, the only predicate appropriate to the manifold of things of
our world (*dokounta*) is that they are beings, or simply that they are.
But this *esti* can then hardly be regarded as predicative *sensu stricto*!

11 Mourelatos (1970: 79-80).

12 Mourelatos (1969: 743-4).

13 Mourelatos (1970: 59).

In view of these disputes, a tendency has emerged in the recent decades to detach the verbal form "Is" from the usual, regular grammatical and syntactical categories. The most prominent example of this tendency is Kahn, whose thesis of a *veridical* "Is"[14] has been discussed for many years. According to this thesis, the Parmenidean "Is" is similar to Wittgenstein's "it is the case": both contain a predicative *and* an existential meaning and refer to the "certain such and such" of every knowable object. But although Kahn succeeded in demonstrating the independent veridical use of "to be" and in distinguishing between the syntactically absolute "veridical construction" and the "veridical nuance" that is constructed with the copula,[15] he was unable to assign convincingly the Parmenidean "Is" to either of these uses. Recognizing this, he would later describe his early attempts as "too schematic."[16] In the end, Kahn dismissed the attempt to identify the Parmenidean "Is" with any of the other uses of "to be" as "naïve": "this conception must ultimately be understood in its own terms, as a metaphysical innovation."[17] In a vein similar to this most welcome verdict are Hölscher's concept of "substantial Being"[18] and the following conclusion by Tugendhat: "what Parmenides meant by 'be' ultimately corresponds to none of the meanings of the word 'be' in our own (or in the Greek) language."[19]

---

14 First presented in Kahn (1969: 711-2).

15 Kahn (1973: 331-37).

16 Kahn (1986: 26).

17 Kahn (1988: 239).

18 Hölscher (1986: 79); cf. also Hölscher (1976: 44): "that something is a being."

19 Tugendhat (1970: 48). The position of Cordero seems similar; he maintains that "*estin* is not impersonal, but it is used by Parmenides as if it were" (2004: 52). Cordero also discerns a "syntactic anomaly" and a "hint of provocation" in the thesis of Parmenides (2004: 62). He rightly views as the crux of that thesis "the presence, the existence,

The Parmenidean "Is" is indeed used in 2.3 absolutively, without a subject or predicate. This *exceptional use*, which cannot be understood by means of the usual grammatical and syntactical categories, is, as it were, a linguistic impertinence, which demonstrates in the best possible manner the radical innovation contained in the now emerging ontology. But such a deviation from the rules of usage of the verb "to be" does not mean that the philosophy of Being has disengaged itself from language altogether. Instead, the emphatic "Is" arises out of a certain "awareness of language,"[20] out of a reflection on the pre-philosophical use of the word "to be" and on the pre-understanding of Being contained in it.

Parmenides' reflection on language neither intends to achieve conformity with its rules, nor does it undertake a blind formalization. In everyday language, "Being" is continually addressed and yet always overlooked and concealed in favor of one or another predication. The unprecedented and surprising Parmenidean use of "Is" refers to that Being that is presupposed by the everyday "is" and that makes possible every predication and every propositional mode, although these take no notice of it. Even though the affirmation of this Being must manifest itself in language, it cannot have its source in language alone. Instead, it presupposes a turn toward Thinking (*noein*). The demand "to say and to think: *eon* is" (6.1) does indeed include Saying within the dimension of Being and Thinking, but the frequent coupling of Saying and Thinking (2.7f., 6.1, 8.8, 8.50) does not justify an equation or identity of the two. The

---

the effectiveness of the fact of being" (ibid.), but then, oddly enough, he ascribes the raising of the question "what is being?" within Greek philosophy to the "overactive imagination of Heidegger" (2004: 60)! Cordero apparently ignores how deeply "Heideggerian" his own reading is, i.e. when he discerns the following one as Parmenides' "essential question": "What is the fact of being that allows there to be beings?" (2004: 155).

20 Schadewaldt (1978: 327).

language to which Parmenides here appeals must be "purified" and, so to speak, ontologically filtered by Thinking: it must cede to the ontological decision made by thought and adapt itself to it. The *logos* of the Aletheia is not a kind of dialectic, but remains after all a "monolectic" that bypasses the multiplicity of everyday language and takes refuge in Thinking. Following Thinking, this *logos* pays attention only to the assertion of "Is" and raises it to the only object of ontology.

Being, Non-Being and their routes are "for thinking," and this means above all: they are not to be seen with the eyes, nor can they ever be experienced through sense perception. Later on (7.3-6), perception is clearly identified as the main source of human error:

> Do not let much-experienced habit force you along that other route, to ply an aimless eye and noisy ear and tongue, but judge by *logos*.

"Aimless" perception, in particular sight, remains fixed on what is present to the senses; it is held captive by them and passes over Being. Thinking, however, proves capable of another view of reality:

> But see through the thought how absent beings are firmly present to it; for [thought] will not cut off *eon* from holding fast to *eon* (4.1-2).

Only Thinking can extend beyond what is immediately given, beyond diremptive perception. Only Thinking can overcome the division into what is present and absent, and even grasp what is "absent" (*apeonta*) as "present" (*pareonta*), i.e. as being (*eonta*), thus recognizing the indivisible connection that binds together everything that is. This is the primary and crucial achievement of Thinking: to no longer accept *apeonta*, but rather to *guarantee the continuity of all that is in a presence that Being alone makes possible.*

The rhetorical turn of phrase "see through the thought (*noos*)" should not mislead us to assume that Parmenides conceives of Thinking (*noein*) and thought (*noos* or *nous*) according to the model of sense perception and its "passive, receptive attitude."[21] Between *noein* and perception one might establish at most a functional analogy. Just as the former is the source of truth, the origin of error lies in the latter. While perception is held captive "passive-receptively" to phenomenality and the interplay between presence and absence, noetic access to Being results from an intellectual exertion that never loses sight of the ontological crossroads, and that therefore always decides in favor of the path of truth.[22]

Thinking is conceived here for the first time as an independent ability to disregard the object's claim to immediate tangibility and to seek out instead a noetic access to the "heart" of reality. The expression "see through the thought" is thus an intentional paradox, which underscores the contrast between perception and Thinking. Being as the only concern of this Thinking is not a substance "out there" that can be receptively taken up, but only becomes manifest as an object of thought. In the final analysis, therefore, there is no reason to raise objections against the translation of the verb *noein* by "to think."[23]

---

21 See, among many others, Heitsch (1974: 99); similarly Wiesner (1996: 27). But already v. Fritz recognized (1945: 43) in the poem of Parmenides "the most important turning-point [...] in the development of the concept of *nous*" in early Greek philosophy.

22 See Thanassas (1997: 66-72).

23 The criticism, raised most frequently by philologists, that such a translation opens the road to "idealism," largely rests on a naïve notion of "idealism." As for the opposite suggestion to translate *noein* as "to know" or "to ascertain," it lends the verb a concretistic nuance which must be reserved for Greek verbs such as *gignôskein*. Parmenidean *noein* does not want to "know," ascertain or identify one or

"Receptivity" characterizes, by contrast, the *nous* of the Doxa, which depends on the "much wandering limbs" and their sense perception; Doxa's *nous* unquestioningly takes up this data and transforms it into "thoughts" (16).

The relation of Thinking to Being is raised in the famous fr. 3, whose potentially "idealistic" implications have generated heated discussions during the past century. "Thinking and Being are the same" is the traditional translation, which has often been vaguely interpreted as "idealism." Because of this, many interpreters have sought refuge in Zeller's old translation: "it is the same thing that can be thought and can be." Controversies surrounding the "correct" grammatical interpretation of the verse arc numerous, and usually pursue the goal of proving the opposing reading as "linguistically impossible." Wiesner, by contrast, has recently shown that although a "complete and total rejection of Zeller's explanation […] cannot be justified" solely on the basis of grammar, the traditional view is nonetheless preferable. As for the equation maintained there, it should be conceived as an "equivalence of concepts related to one another."[24] Heidegger's interpretation leads to a similar result. He seizes upon the original sense of *to auto* and interprets the "sameness" as the "belonging together" of Being and Thinking.[25]

---

another thing as this or that, but to "think" and affirm their unitary Being. Apart from this, the fact that the second route is an essential object of *noein* (2.5) but not an object of any knowledge whatsoever (2.7) makes in our eyes the translation of *noein* as "to know" impossible.

24 See Wiesner's balanced and philologically definitive analysis (1996: 139-49). Giancola's (2001) exhaustive and persuasive argumentation against numerous supporters of Zeller's reading results finally in an unnecessary, unfortunate support of a "religious-mystical" interpretation.

25 Two of many instances can be found in Heidegger (1954: 147) and (1957: 18).

Indeed, the relation of Being and Thinking should not be taken as a mathematical identity, in which either term can be replaced with the other – for this would deprive them both of their distinctive character. The kind of link between Being and Thinking is specified in fr. 3 by the double force of *te kai*, which suggests an interaction, a *mutual connection and reciprocal reference*: no Thinking without Being, no Being without Thinking. This second aspect was formulated in fr. 2, where the route of Being and its emphatic "Is" were explicitly presented as "for thinking," i.e. as an achievement of Thinking. The first aspect appears for its part in 8.35-6: "without *eon* you will not find Thinking." Being that is thought is therefore not something simply made up, not an arbitrarily chosen object of Thinking, but what emerges together with the activity of thought. If thought were not directed to Being, it would lose its compass, revert to perception's dead-ends and thereby lose its noetic character altogether.

Thus, while fr. 3 in its traditional interpretation articulates the main task of Thinking, i.e. its tie to Being, Zeller's interpretation allows the dissociation of Being and Thinking and transforms the fragment into an assertion of one-sided dependence: "Only that can be thought which can be,"[26] but also "only that can be which can be thought."[27] Zeller's reading of fr. 3 imputes to Parmenides a fatal ambiguity in the determination of the relation between Being and Thinking. Moreover, closer inspection reveals that the two possibilities permitted by this interpretation cannot be reconciled with Parmenides' conception of truth. In the "realistic" reduction of Thinking to "what can be," Being is shifted to the domain of the possible and released

---

26 For this "realistic" rendering, see Zeller (³1869: 470).

27 This was the case in Zeller (²1856: 398). This version, obviously, can only give support to the "idealism" it is meant to undermine. Surprisingly, even Hölscher (1968: 97) decided in favor of this latter view, although he also wanted to reject "idealism."

from the "bonds of necessity" (8.30-1) that hold it and that
are intended to ban Non-Being. Even less acceptable is the dependence of "what can be" on "what can be thought," which
amounts to reducing Being to an ego-centered subjective idealism.

As long as the ambiguity and the vagueness in the notion
of "idealism" remain, it will be difficult to agree on its appropriateness and justification in the context of the poem. In any
case, Parmenidean "idealism" should never be confused with
a modern form of idealism like Berkeley's *esse est percipere*.[28] It
was certainly *not* Parmenides' intention to make Thinking the
measure of what could possibly be, nor did he intend to raise
the question (foreign to Greek thought) of the *realitas* of what
is. Parmenidean "idealism" would also not eliminate the plurality of the world in favor of a new object, like that of a second,
"intelligible world." It is not ontic reality, but only Being, that
here becomes the "same" as Thinking. The "Is" contains an ontology "drawn by *nous* from the things" themselves,[29] in order
to grasp the world of appearances "as beings" and in this way to
"save" them.

The relation of Being and Thinking is again articulated in the
equally controversial line 8.34:

> Thinking and [Being as] the cause of thought are the same.

The concordance with fr. 3 has occasionally been challenged,[30]
and this phrase has even served as an occasion for dismissing
the authenticity of fr. 3.[31] If we follow again the traditional
opinion and see here the verse as syntactically analogous to fr.
3, then the ambiguity of the word *houneken* can be interpret-

---

28 Parmenides is seen as a forerunner of Berkeley in the interpretation of
    Barnes (1982: 170-1).

29 See Buchheim (1994: 117).

30 Hölscher (1968: 100).

31 Manchester (1979: 97), Gadamer (GW 7: 20).

ed as another signal of the reciprocal mediation of Being and Thinking, one which Parmenides may even have intended. If *houneken* is read as "on the grounds of," Being appears as the foundation of Thinking; if it is taken as "for the sake of," Being appears rather as Thinking's task and goal.

To the same context belongs a further elucidation of the relation between Being and Thinking at 8.35-6a: "for without *eon*, to which it stands committed, you will not find Thinking."[32] Thinking's bond with Being is then justified once again in the following passage (36b-37a), which has come down to us in two disparate versions. The generally accepted version is in itself unmetrical and trivializes the passage,[33] while the second is hardly tenable in its content.[34] Perhaps we should therefore resuscitate an old conjecture of Stein,[35] which not only explains the divergence of the textual variants, but above all makes excellent sense: "no necessity is or will be apart from *eon*." The

---

32 The parenthetical statement *en hô pephatismenon estin* and the notion of Thinking as "spoken out" *in* Being have often irritated commentators: It is actually Being that lets itself be "spoken out" in Thinking, and not the reverse. We think that what is intended here is not a narrowly understood spatial relation, but Thinking's affiliation and attachment to Being. As something meaningful (*pephatismenon*), Thinking must remain "contained" in and assigned to Being. In this translation we follow Mourelatos (1970: 171-2). But is also worth considering the philosophically less challenging suggestion of Stokes, who takes the relative sentence merely as a reference back to what had been presented before by the goddess: "in the state in which I have described it" (1971: 314).

33 *ouden gar <ê> estin ê estai allo parex tou eontos*, «for nothing else is or will be apart from Being», Simpl. *In Phys.* 86.

34 *oud' ei chronos...*: «even if time is or will be something other than Being», Simpl. *In Phys.* 146. – I had decided in favor of this variant in Thanassas (1997: 125-6), but now hold this reading to be untenable.

35 *ouden chreos...*, Simpl. *In Phys.* 146.

concept of necessity would be introduced again here as the compelling condition of a Thinking that seeks the truth and for that reason is directed again and again to Being as its only necessary and sufficient counterpart.

4

THE SIGNS OF BEING

Fragment 8, the longest of all fragments preserved, begins with a new allusion to the "route of Being." Following the rejection of Non-Being and of the so-called "third way" in fr. 7, this route manifests itself now as the only route that really merits a detailed "account" of the goddess:

> And on it there are signs very many: that *eon* is ungenerated and imperishable, whole and unique, unshaken and complete (8.2-4).

Parmenides will flesh out this program in the following verses, which delineate the different characteristics of *eon* in detail. Of paramount importance here is the question of the intended sense and the status of the participial form *eon*, which appears repeatedly in the poem alongside the purely verbal form "Is" (*estin*). Does *eon* denote a single, uniquely existing, huge, and robust entity that negates the multiplicity of the world? Heidegger has called attention to the dual employment of this participle, which incorporates not only a nominal ("a something that is") but also a verbal sense ("the Being of that which is").[1] He finds in this congruence support for the thesis that already with Parmenides philosophy lapses into the famous "forgetfulness of Being" and becomes unable to establish a clear distinction between Being and entities. Against this position, how-

---

1 See Heidegger (1954: 133). This duality actually pertains to all participles and establishes the basis of this grammatical category, which lies between noun and verb.

ever, we would insist that Parmenides uses *eon* exclusively in its verbal sense, conceiving it thus in a complete semantic equivalence to the verb *estin*.[2]

Understanding *eon* nominally ("a being") commits us to asserting that only this entity exists, while the plurality in the world is denied. This position, however, is implausible, if only for the simple reason that the Aletheia frequently mentions a plurality of *eonta* (4.1-2, 8.25, 8.47-8). On the other hand, a verbal employment of *eon*, which amounts to its *semantic identity and synonymy* with *estin*, can be observed at several points throughout the poem.[3] In 6.1-2 the assertion "*eon* is" is grounded by again taking up the first route (*esti einai*), and in 7.1 the route of Non-Being comes to be formulated by way of the expression "nonbeings are." In particular, the very announcement of *sêmata* (8.1-2) demonstrates that, strictly speaking, these are not signs of *eon* but rather belong to the "route of Being." The following account of these signs will have the intention of enabling movement along this route, while the concept of *eon* only serves to secure for the route a specific determination. This is why the major "decision" (*krisis*) between *estin* and *ouk estin* is invoked again (8.15-8) during the account of *eon*.

Drawing on a distinction from modern logic, we could identify *eon* "extensionally" with the totality of appearing entities. Yet if we view it "intensionally," with regard to its conceptual content, *eon* appears as distinct from this totality. Its verbal

---

2   Shorey (1900: 206-9), Beaufret (1955: 39), Tarán (1965: 37), Wiesner (1996: 81) and Cordero (2004: 100) all argue for such semantic equivalence. Kahn has also stressed that "the infinitive and participle serve merely as a convenient nominalization of the indicative *esti*" (1973: 191). – Similarly to Parmenides, the Heraclitean participle *to katheudon* (DK22 B88) is not to be understood as "that which sleeps," but rather as "the sleeping of what sleeps."

3   The same is the case with *ouk estin* and *mê eon*, which are also used as synonyms.

significance does not simply encompass the totality of entities by adding them together, but rather takes their Being into its scope. It is precisely this second aspect that predominates in the Parmenidean use of *eon*. The participle names neither the indeterminate totality of (nominally understood) entities nor a massive "block" of Being in the sense of some enormous, unworldly and wonderful structure that would count as the only true existent. It emerges as a conceptual formulation out of the thinking of the verb *estin* and makes possible an account of its characteristics. Parmenidean *eon* is thus directly comparable to the Aristotelian expression *on hê on*, in that it denotes the totality of entities (in the first *on* of this expression), but also (most importantly, in the second *on* of the expression) calls attention to the Being of those entities. In its verbal character, *eon* is semantically identical to *einai*, so that both should be translated as "Being."

This (exclusively verbal) employment of the participle *eon* testifies to an immense and far-reaching accomplishment in concept formation.[4] Its significance is perhaps best viewed in relation to the *physiologoi*, whose innovations Parmenides steers in a radically new direction. For them, "water" and "air" still oscillate between their rational function and their role as material components of the world. In the same vein, the *archê* to which they appealed only offered an "origin" and a "ruling" ground of the world because it essentially remained a component of this world. Like those previous attempts, the Parmenidean *to eon* also draws on the determining function of the grammatical article, which (particularly in the nominalization of participles) determines the universal and establishes it as an object of statements.[5] But this formal resemblance ought not to cover over the radical transformation effected in the poem. Similar to the *physiologoi*, Parmenides refers to the one world

---

4 Cf. Gadamer (GW 7: 21).

5 Cf. Snell (1953: 231-2).

of phenomena. But prior to the question "what is everything?" that was animating the mythical cosmogonies as well as the Ionian philosophers, and was leading them to posit the origin of the world-order in water, air, or fire, Parmenides' Aletheia poses at the forefront another question: "Is or Is-not?" Through this ingenious replacement of the "What?" by the simple affirmation of the "That," the unity sought in all philosophical approaches can now be detected in Being, which underlies all phenomena.

⧲

The account of the *first* sign (8.5-21), more extensive than the following three, begins with a reference to time, and then introduces its actual theme with two questions:

> Nor was [*eon*] before, nor will it be, since it is now all together, one, continuous. For what birth could you seek for it? How and whence did it grow? (8.5-7a).

This no doubt intentional intertwining of becoming and time, which anticipates the explicit correlation of change (or movement) and time in Aristotle,[6] is perhaps unexpected of Parmenides. Moreover, his own position on time remains highly controversial: Does he want to deny any form of temporality whatsoever, or only the generation of *eon* in the past and its perishing in the future?[7] The discussion among interpreters has largely been carried out under the keywords of *eon*'s "perpetual duration" and "atemporal eternity."[8] However, the dependency of these terms on the scholastic and theologically overburdened concepts of *aeternitas* and *sempiternitas* should raise doubts about how appropriate they are here.

---

6 Cf. *Phys.* 219b 1-2.

7 The latter option was first advanced by Fränkel (1955: 46).

8 Cf. Tarán (1979), Owen (1966), Theunissen (1991).

Parmenides' crucial intention is to stress the irrelevance of the unfolding of time into past, present, and future for his ontological project. Being is not "in time"; it has no history and no future (8.20). If *eon* is "all together, one, continuous," if it remains unavailable to any kind of change, then any question of a past and a future becomes superfluous and redundant. The affirmation of time suggested by "perpetual duration" (*sempiternitas*) thus proves unsuited to Parmenidean Being – as does the utter negation of every temporality implied by "atemporal eternity" (*aeternitas*). Attributing "now' (*nyn*, 8.5) to Being, however, only seemingly arrays *eon* in temporal relations. If time is experienced only in close connection with change, and if we bear in mind the disavowal of generation and perishing announced by the phrase "all together, one, continuous," *nyn* cannot be temporal. Similar to the Heraclitean and Empedoclean *aiôn*, this *nyn* seems to suggest a quasi non-temporal mode of time, which transcends the traditional trinity of "was – is – will be." Or else, it remains a figurative, non-literal temporal determination, which stresses the *irrelevance of temporality for ontology*.

The subsequent text treats the two questions previously posed (6b-7a) and the two distinct modes of development indicated by them. The section 7b-11 undertakes the proof of the impossibility of *eon*'s "birth," i.e. its generation *in toto*:

> From Non-Being I shall not allow you to say or to think [that *eon* was born]; for it is impossible to say or to think that Is-not [*ouk esti*]; what necessity would have impelled it later or sooner to take its birth from Nothing? Thus it is necessary either to be completely or not at all.

Obviously enough, this reasoning succeeds here on the basis of the insights previously established. Since there are only two routes constituting the ontological framework, the origin of *eon*'s generation could only be located in Non-Being. Thinking, knowing and communicability once again provide the

testing instances for the evaluation and denial of such generation *ex nihilo*, and "necessity" (*chreos*) is once more stipulated as
an indispensable component of any ontology. The disavowal of
an origin foreign to *eon* demonstrates its complete and uninterrupted presence; for even the slightest breach would lead to the
utter dissolution of *eon*. This Being bears no shading, for that
could only be brought about by Nothing. It is not "more here,
less there" (8.23-4). It is either fully or not at all.

This insight allows for the transition to a second possibility,
i.e. an "increase" of *eon*, in the sense of a partial development
distinct from the absolute "birth" previously denied:

> Nor will the force of conviction ever permit that out of
> Non-Being something arises [i.e. is added] alongside Being
> (12-13a).[9]

The singularity of Being and its fullness forecloses in advance
any growth out of itself and focuses the investigation upon
an "external" cause. The question concerning the "whence" of
growth thus necessarily leads to a reconsideration and a prompt
refusal of the abstruse thought of an active, generative Non-
Being. But the question "whither?" would likewise prove to be
absurd, since *eon* has always already attained its wholeness and
has divested itself of every development, including the kind
of development associated with increase, accumulation, or any
growth whatsoever.

Individual beings certainly wax and wane, submitted to the
ceaseless sequence of becoming and perishing. Parmenides
would hardly dispute this. In fact, he will later make becoming
and perishing the theme of the longest part of his poem (cf.

---

9 By coordinating this passage with the second of the originally posited
   questions ("how and whence did it grow?"), the traditional conjecture is rendered superfluous, according to which "out of Non-Being"
   (*ek mê eontos*) should be changed into "out of Being," thus either to
   ek tou eontos (Reinhardt 1916: 42) or to *ek dê eontos* (Hölscher 1986:
   20).

19). In the Aletheia, however, the signs on the route of Being do not pertain to particular entities *per se*, but only to their Being as such. Only this Being can claim to be exempt from every kind of change and to eliminate continually its nugatory counterpart Non-Being. In the role of *eon*'s protector will shortly appear "Justice" (*Dike*), who

> has not allowed it to come to be nor to perish by loosening the fetters, but holds firm (8.13b-15a).

More important than this divine assertion, however, seems to be the ontological guarantee won only by thinking the irreconcilable antithesis between both routes:

> The decision about these matters lies in this: either Is or Is-not. Now it has been decided, just as is necessary, to abandon one route as unthinkable and nameless, for it is not true, while the other route –that Is– is true (15b-18).

Finally, the relation between becoming and threefold time is again brought to mind before the goddess triumphantly proclaims the accomplishment of the goal intended in this sign:

> How could *eon* perish later on?[10] How could it come to be? For if it came to be, it is not, nor if it is going to be in the future. Thus coming-to-be is extinguished and perishing is unheard of (19-21).

Coming-to-be always results from what-is-not-yet, while perishing is a passing into no-longer-being; both must be ruled out, since they effectively situate Non-Being alongside Being in the domain of ontology.

After the extrinsic relation of *eon* to Nothing has been treated, and every possibility of coming-to-be as well as any externally

---

10 I read at this point with DK *epeit' apoloito* and not *epeita peloi to* ("be only later").

effected development has been ruled out, the *second* of the signs
turns to the intrinsic constitution of *eon*:

> Nor is it divisible, since it [*eon*] is all alike; nor is it some-
> what more here, which would prevent it from holding to-
> gether, and somewhat less there, but everything is full of
> Being [*eon*]. Therefore everything is continuous: Being con-
> sorts with Being (8.22-5).

Divisibility would be a necessary precondition for a differenti-
ated depiction of *eon*'s inner constitution. Only on this basis
could one seek to discover divergences in its various fields or
"domains." *Eon* proves, however, to be "indivisible," which not
only makes factual division impossible, but also utterly denies
the very possibility of any rupture or opening-up in general.
It has no parts and exhibits no quantitative or qualitative di-
versity, it cannot be here "less" (or "poorer," *cheiroteron*) than
it is there. If everything is "seen" (i.e. is thought) not as this
or that, but exclusively "as being," then no distinctions can
be discerned, no internal bounds can be drawn, and no parts
can be distinguished. No longer is each thing considered in its
particular determinacy, but is instead placed into the uniform
perspective of Being and is grasped only as being: "*eon* consorts
with *eon*," and this dense cohesion establishes the thoroughgo-
ing and indissoluble interconnection of all reality.

This is certainly not a *physical analysis*, but an *ontological account* of reality in light of the basic distinction between Being
and Non-Being. The continuity that fills the universe is neither
present to hand nor sensibly perceptible. It is attained only by
thought, insofar as it disregards the respective constitutions of
individual entities and grasps only what it is common to them,
i.e. the fact that they *are*. The expression calling everything "full
of *eon*" does not necessarily reject the void in the physical sense
of the term, but rather denotes an *ontological plentitude* that
has nothing in common with physical spatiality, emptiness, or
mass. On the field established by both routes any ontological

differentiation and gradation would be possible only as a result of an admixture of Non-Being. Hence Being may exhibit no gradations or degrees. It is internally symmetrical and "alike" (*homoion*) and, since it is a unified "whole" and "unique" (*oulon, mounogenes*, 8.4), it must demonstrate a generic, homogeneous monotony.

Instead of outlawing boundaries internal to *eon*, the *third* sign will bring the preceding two together by showing that a limit external to it is not only possible, but indispensable for the inner stability discussed above:

> And so, unmovable within the limits of great bonds, it is without beginning or end, since coming-to-be and perishing have been banished far away: true conviction has thrust them out. The same and remaining in the same, it lies by itself and so will remain there firm; for strong necessity holds it within the bonds of the limit which fences it about (8.26-31).

Whereas the first sign raised the issue of *eon*'s temporality, it is now the spatial aspect that comes into the foreground. The firm limit (*peiras*) secures the immobility of *eon* and delimits it – not as an ordinary boundary, which determines an extended thing in space, but rather as an ontological limit, which everywhere in reality divides Being from Non-Being and accomplishes the paradoxical task of fending off the specter of Nothingness.

The reference to the outcome of the first sign and the reminder that, since *eon* is ungenerated and imperishable, it is also "without beginning or end," ground its immobility exclusively upon the fact that it has no relation to Non-Being. This ontological argument against motion[11] by no means denies the movement of individual things in the world of appearances – a subject brought up explicitly later, in the Doxa section of the poem. It excludes only the kind of ontological "movement" which makes Being approach Nothing and become mixed with

---

11 Cf. Kirk/Stokes (1960).

the latter. *Eon* shares with the "heart of truth" the quality of be-ing "unshaken" (1.29 and 8.4), since this "heart" is filled only with Being and beats only for its affirmation. This feature of being "unshaken" goes beyond the "immobility" that simply rejected any external relation to Non-Being and any transition to it; it proves immobility to be the outcome of the "sameness" of *eon*, which tarries "in the same" place since it remains identi-cal to itself. This earliest philosophical articulation of the con-cept of identity does not exclude difference but rather includes it. It does not reject plurality and the manifold of appearances, but it rather allows them to appear within the unifying per-spective of an identical Being and forces divergent Non-Being to dissolve into indeterminate disparity.

The *fourth* sign (8.32-3 and 42-9) demonstrates the perfec-tion and completeness of *eon*:

> Wherefore it is not right for *eon* to be incomplete; for it is not in need: if it were, it would lack everything. But since there is an outermost limit, it is completed from every side, like the body of a well-rounded sphere, equally strong every-where from the center – for it may not be more or less, here or there. For neither is there Non-Being to prevent it from reaching its like, nor is *eon* such that it might be here more and there less than *eon*, since it is all inviolate. Equal thus to itself from everywhere, it uniformly lies within its limits.[12]

It is with the discussion of the perfection of *eon* that the signs reach their culmination. The "aim" or "end" (*telos*) indicated by the perfect tense "completed" (*tetelesmenon*) is not the conse-

---

12 These verses are interrupted by the passage 8.34-41, which recapitu-lates the most important conclusions of the Aletheia section of the poem. According to a convincing view of Ebert (1989), this passage was placed there only because of a transcriber's error. This opinion gains in plausibility if the original, proper place of 8.34-41 is located not after 8.52 (as Ebert thought), but rather after 8.49 (cf. Barnes 1982: 180 and Thanassas 1997: 104).

quence of an energetic accomplishment nor of a gradual procedure; it is rather a status always already attained, insofar and so
long as one proceeds thoughtfully along the route of Being.[13]
The "limit" asserted here once again gives *eon* its closure and
frees it from the defect of being incomplete or impending. The
Greek ideal of perfection, the preference for measured comple-
tion rather than infinite progress, is here given its ontological
foundation in an utter self-sufficiency of Being that does not let
even the smallest "need" arise.

That "limit" is "outermost" since it indeed surpasses every
other conceivable limit. It does not divide regions of reality,
but embraces the entirety of the real and protects it from the
only outcast, i.e. Non-Being. Within this limit, *eon* remains
"completed from every side," and this condition is promptly
compared to a "well-rounded sphere." Simplicius had already
recognized the metaphorical character of the image,[14] and this
view now prevails, in opposition to interpretations that hold
eon literally to possess the form of a geometrical sphere. The
text makes clear that *eon* is merely "like" a sphere and that the
tertium comparationis is its comprehensive perfection.[15] The
function of the comparison, which is suggested by the Greek
appreciation of circles and spheres as the most perfect geometrical figures, is further concretized by the subsequent statement
depicting *eon* as "equally strong everywhere from the centre."
The point of reference for the sphere-image is the surface of the
sphere, on which alone all points stand in the selfsame relation
to the center.

---

13 In the same sense ("not first to bring to a goal") is *ateleston* to be
understood, in the announcement of this sign (8.4). Otherwise the
conjecture to *teleston* ("complete") becomes necessary (see on this
Tarán 1965: 93-5).

14 Cf. *In Phys.* 143.1 ff.

15 Cf. in particular Mourelatos (1970: 126) and Heitsch (1974: 175);
alternately Bormann (1971: 175) and Sedley (1999: 121).

It becomes clear that only the outer shape of the sphere is important and not its internal mass.[16] Moreover, if the surface area of the sphere is also understood to be the limit, then the following may be stated: Just as the sphere is equally bounded and determined by its surface, so too does the limit of Being allow all appearances to be understood as equivalent – that is, "as beings." This equivalence is then immediately established by an explicit recourse to Being and Nothing; *eon* is not hindered by Non-Being from "reaching its like," and is thus always already by itself and with itself, in a condition of complete fullness of Being that makes it "inviolate." Again, this is not a religious quality, but rather the consequence of an ontological insight. Since all distinctions and gradations of Being are recognized to be effects of Non-Being, they are altogether rejected. Being, therefore does not admit of "more or less."

The length of the eighth fragment, its tight construction and the thoroughness of its discussion of the signs have often provoked interpreters to regard this text more or less as the heart of Parmenidean philosophy. Yet such an overemphasis would contradict the character of any sign whatsoever – for "a sign is nothing but what its function requires; and that function is to point away from itself." That this thesis of Gadamer[17] holds for Parmenides' poem is demonstrated by the explicit introduction of signs in 8.1-2 as path markers, which one encounters *along* the route of Being – that is, only *after* one has already found this route and entered onto it. The function of these signs is not to substitute for Being itself, to suppress or oust it; rather,

---

16 Mourelatos (1970: 126) argues convincingly that *ogkos* here denotes nothing but the "shape" of the sphere.

17 Gadamer (GW 1: 157); see also the English transl.: *Truth and Method*, [2]1989: 145.

they are supposed to direct attention away from themselves and toward what they "designate." They are not intended to introduce some new strange entity called *eon* and place it in the foreground, but to act as warnings against any derailment from the route of Being. They all operate not so much as positive attributes but rather as *negative marks fending off any encroachment of Non-Being.*

In contrast to the later Aristotelian ontology, which thematizes "being *qua* being and what belongs to it,"[18] Parmenidean ontology has as its object "being *qua* being and what is missing from it." Generation and growth, threefold temporality and plurality, division and differentiation, movement and openness: these are conceived within this ontology as implicit concessions to Non-Being and must therefore be excluded. But even the signs that appear positive at first sight, those of totality and identity, continuity or perfection, function primarily as rejections of the presence of Non-Being within the concepts of division and difference, of discontinuity and gradual fulfillment.

An explicit choice in favor of Non-Being was already proscribed in fr. 2 because of its lack of intelligibility and communicability. If later on Parmenides repeatedly returns to Non-Being, he does so above all with regard to its *implicit* presence in human opinions and in the explanatory models of the Ionians. Human opinions are set out and scrutinized not only in the Doxa (8.54-9), but also within the Aletheia (frs. 6, 7). The critical discussion of the cosmogonies and cosmologies of Ionian (or mythical) origin is for its part accomplished in the context of the signs of Being (8.1-49). It is here, in the eighth fragment, that we could seek a Parmenidean polemic against other philosophies, and not in the Doxa section. Thus when Parmenides describes *eon* as "not somewhat more here [...] and somewhat less there," he is likely aiming at Anaximenes, who

---

18 *Met.*1003a 21-2.

wants to derive everything from the "rarefaction" (*araiôsis*) and the "condensation" (*pyknôsis*) of air. Altogether, the "signs" fulfill the purpose of showing that the categories of traditional cosmogony as well as of everyday life-experience are vehicles for Non-Being and must consequently be barred from entering the ontology now coming to light.

The task of the signs is therefore *rhetorically and dialectically determined*, and this fact not only explains the distinctive negativity of the fragment, but also accounts for the fact that contested categories are occasionally employed in a way that divests them of their ordinary meaning. If *eon*, for example, is "now" (8.6) or "will remain there firm" (8.30), this mode of speaking in no way implies a classification of *eon* into the traditional categories of space and time. Such quasi-temporal and quasi-spatial determinations should not be allowed to obscure the fact that *eon* is not at all in time, that it refrains from any becoming, avoids all change, and "is now all together, one, continuous." By the same token, it does not allow itself to be located in a determinate place, but embraces all appearances and integrates them into an all-present abundance, excluding from itself only Non-Being.

In order to demonstrate the incompatibility of the cosmogonic and cosmological models with his own ontological project, Parmenides, in the eighth fragment, occasionally applies their own conceptual schemata so as to show their weakness in light of the truth of Being. The ambivalence of this enterprise and the terminology he occasionally employs in the poem seem to suggest that the signs of Being "have a cosmological impact."[19] We would like to insist, however, that the cosmological impact of the doctrine of Being only comes about in post-Parmenidean cosmology.[20] In the poem itself, the only cosmological implications of the Aletheia lie in its *resolute elimination and destruction*

---

19 Gadamer (GW 6: 37); cf. also Hölscher (1986: 100-1).

20 Cf. in particular Boeder (1994: 117-69).

of all traditional cosmological schemata. If we compare Being to an Ionic "principle" (*archê*), for example, we will find not only that Being is not a principle, but furthermore that the question of an *archê* in general becomes obsolete within ontology. In this field, which is free from all change and becoming, and in the uninterruptedly uniform presence of the one Being, there can be no question of an origin of becoming or of an underlying ground of all change. This was noticed early on, as when Aristotle writes that "there is no longer a principle, if only one [thing...] is. For a principle is always principle *of* something, one or more."[21]

But was Parmenides for this reason a "monist"? A crude doctrine admitting the existence of "only one thing" would be incompatible with certain passages in the poem that treat of more than one being,[22] beginning with the very first declaration of truth (1.32), which demands grasping the plurality of appearances (*dokounta*) "as beings." Rendering Parmenidean "monism" with the thesis "all is one" remains ambivalent as well: If it does not merely draw attention to the (in fact trivial) insight that every totality first becomes visible as such from within a unifying perspective, it tends to impute to Parmenides a denial of plurality and a fixation on "the One." Against this, it is worth recalling that the poem treats not "the One" but rather Being, that Parmenides does not pursue a *henology but rather an ontology*; and further, that "one" occurs only once in the preserved fragments (8.6), as a determination of what is alone relevant, namely Being. Aristotle is generally quite critical of Parmenides, but he clearly distinguishes him from Xenophanes and the genuinely "monistic" Melissus. In fact, it is precisely by identifying the underlying ontological reason for the unity of Parmenides' Being that Aristotle is able to judge him superior to those crude monists. In contrast to these thinkers, "Par-

---

21 *Phys.* 185a 3-5.

22 Cf. below, p. 58, n. 24.

menides seems to speak with more insight; since he maintains
that next to Being Non-Being is not, he necessarily believes
that Being is one."[23]

Only because the ontological inquiry moves exclusively between Being and Non-Being as the "only" (*mounai*) routes,
is it necessary that Being remains the one and only outcome
of the noetic "decision" (*krisis*) and that *eon* be identified as
"one." This *eon* is no huge, all-encompassing, spatially extended "block" that exists all by itself, but rather a *precise, compact
reconstruction of the world of appearances made possible by the
noetic form of Being.* The Parmenidean ontological determinations occur in the plural[24] as well as in the singular form.[25] This
lack of differentiation may lend strength to the notion that,
in contrast to Heraclitus, the dialectical problem of unity and
plurality has not yet been seen by Parmenides. Yet, at the same
time, it shows that the object domain of the singular *eon* is
not to be sought in a Beyond, but simply in the really existing
world. Parmenidean Being does not abolish the plurality we
discover in this worldly existence. It takes it up into ontology
and preserves it there. As for the ontological unity, this does
not first come about in fr. 8 with the "one *eon*," but is already
accomplished in fr. 4 by Thinking, insofar as it views the many
absent things as "present" and thus inserts them into the unify-

---

23 *Met.* 986b 27-9. For the imaginative construction of an "Eleatic
    School" and for the occasionally devastating influence of this in-
    vention on understanding Parmenidean philosophy, see Thanassas
    (1997: 256-67).

24 1.32: *dokounta* qua *onta*; 4.1: *noô pareonta*; 4.2: *eon eontos echesthai*;
    8.25: *eon eonti pelazei.* – The only interpreter who has called atten-
    tion to these expressions is Steiger (1986: 199-201), who concludes
    that "Parmenides refers also to the parts of *eon* with the expression
    eon." The reason for this dual usage, according to Steiger, is a pro-
    found duality of *eon*, which indicates "the universe as a whole" but
    also "the whole of the parts of the universe."

25 *to einai, to eon.*

ing perspective of Being present in Thinking. The "very many" signs along the route of Being would be impossible, if the unity of the *eon* they determine strove to exclude every plurality. But taken as secondary determinations, which point away from Non-Being and toward the route of Being, they are certainly compatible with Parmenidean "monism." After all, this "monism," in making visible the unity of Being as an accomplishment of thought, does not exclude the plurality of appearances, but instead includes it.

The plurality of signs, accordingly, does not testify to an "internal self-contradiction" in the doctrine of Being.[26] Nevertheless, their legitimacy is not immediately convincing. If Being and Non-Being emerge only in Thinking, if only the emphatic affirmation of "Is" adheres to truth, while every other manner of speaking is relegated to the Doxa, then what is the justification of these signs qua determinations of thought that are distinct from Being? Perhaps it would have been more consistent with his ontological monism if Parmenides had limited himself to the simple affirmation of Being and of its unconditional immanence. By introducing the signs, he took a step away from the "monolectic" of Being towards a quasi-dialectical procedure[27] and to a pluralistic *logos*, which expresses itself in a manifold of determinations without thereby being able to offer an account of them.

---

26 As Gadamer thought (GW 6: 19).

27 Cf. Boeder (1994: 109-10).

5

DOXA: MIXTURE VS. PARTITION

The plan and the content of Doxa, the second and longest part of the poem, are outlined in fr. 10:[1]

> You shall know the generation of aether and all aetherial signs and the destructive works of the splendid sun's pure torch, and whence they came to be. And you shall learn the wandering works of the round-faced moon and her generation, and you shall also know the surrounding heaven, whence it was born and how necessity led and fettered it to hold the limits of the stars.[2]

Similarly, fr. 11 promises to describe in detail

> how earth and sun and moon and the common aether and the heavenly galaxy and Olympus the outermost and the hot power of the stars strove eagerly to come to be.

Both these programmatic announcements and the (admittedly sparse) verses that testify to the accomplishment of this program are often overshadowed by that initial passage of the Doxa section, wherein the goddess notes that the story she will now tell is a "deceitful" one:

---

1 Bicknell maintains that this fragment follows directly the proemium (1968: 631). – This chapter and the first part of the following one draw on material published in Thanassas (2005) and Thanassas (2006).

2 On the meaning of *physis* as "generation" and on the obvious "rigorously drawn parallelism" of cosmogony *qua* "generation" and cosmology *qua* current "works," see Heinimann (1945: 90-1).

> Here I end for you my convincing account and thought
> about truth. From here onwards learn mortal opinions, lis-
> tening to the deceitful ordering of my words (8.50-2).

The word *apatêlos*, "deceitful" or "deceptive," is *the* stumbling
block for every interpretation of Doxa, since it seems incompatible both with the status of the goddess as the goddess of
truth as well as with her promise to introduce a positive learning process (*manthane*). The use of the word "deceitful" obviously places the status of Doxa in doubt, but the riddle is
exacerbated when this adjective is contrasted with the subsequent announcement of the goddess eight verses later, where
she promises to present the whole world-arrangement as an
"*appearing*" or "*appropriate*" one (8.60).[3] Every serious attempt
to interpret Doxa thus has to expose itself to the full brunt of
the tension between the divine proclamations of an "appropriate" representation of the world and the announcement of a
deceptive speech.[4] The recognition of this tension is certainly

---

3 These are the only senses of the word *eoikôs* possible at that time,
   distinct from the later sense of the sophistical agonistic practice of
   "probable speech" (*eoikotes logoi*). The divine representation does not
   come to be accepted owing to some rhetorical aptitude, but rather
   becomes binding and is "appropriate" because it does justice to the
   real order of the world as it appears. The translation of the word
   with "probable," a practice that rests on the older hypothetical interpretations of the Doxa (s. above, p. 19-20), is furthermore hardly
   compatible with the subsequent explanation of the divine intent: "so
   that no mortal view may ever outstrip you" (8.61). In contrast to this
   categorically unsurpassable character, a merely "probable" presentation would imply a gradation of knowledge; it would be permanently
   endangered, for a "more probable" one could always exceed it.

4 Hölscher has most obviously dedicated himself to this task. In his interpretation, Doxa is designated as a grey area between the deceptive
   and the adequate, between explanation and deceit, described finally
   as a "half-truth" (1986: 103). Despite its unquestionable merit, this
   interpretation stands in our view as a significant hermeneutic capitu-
   lation to the obstacles that arise in the attempt to define the status

preferable to the one-sided emphasis on the "deceptive" character of Doxa and to its subsequent depreciation. But a different, admittedly uncommon approach might prove even more promising: a view of the Doxa section not as a homogeneous unity but rather as a complex, within which *various and diverse interests, purposes and intentions* are articulated and fulfilled.[5]

---

of Doxa as a unique totality. Sensitivity to the "puzzles" posed by the Doxa section has also been recently shown by Curd (1998: 100-4). For his part, and with a refreshing straightforwardness, Hermann has reminded us that "if we dismiss Doxa as a fraud, there is nothing to stop us from invalidating it entirely, meaning we will have to equate it with that which is not, or to nonexistence. [...] no scholar who supports this view has been able to explain why the account of Mortal Opinion is included in the Poem if it is so hopelessly deceptive" (2004: 169, 173).

5   On the following see also Thanassas (1997: 160-70). A similar account is given by Scuto, who describes his Doxa-interpretation as being in conformity with some "newest commentaries" (2005: 114-5), but without specific references. Finkelberg has also rejected the denunciation of Doxa as erroneous, but his account of *apatêlos* as indicating a "plausible narrative" (1999: 242) disregards its negative force and is hardly convincing. In his most recent analysis, Nehamas (2002: 58) stipulates too that Parmenides "believes both that mortal opinions are deceptive and that his cosmology is correct." But despite his proclamation that "the Doxa is Parmenides' glory," he falls back to the traditional deadlocks of the era before Reinhardt, when he concludes that "though accurate, [Doxa] is a description of appearance and thus a description of a *false* world, and that's why he warns us against it" (2002: 62-3). But what does it mean for it to be a "*false* world," what are the ontological presuppositions and the epistemological implications of this peculiar expression and of the enigmatic possibility of a "correct description of the wrong thing"? In any case, Nehamas' interpretation does not seem to us so "revolutionary" (and its merits so "unprecedented") as celebrated by Hermann (2004: 178). Robbiano (2006: 224) also asserts that *eoikôs* "corrects the negative impression" evoked by *apatêlos* but does not explain how this is possible and in what sense it takes place.

This means that we should first of all consider the possibility that the term "deceitful" refers *only* to the passage immediately following (8.53-9):

> For they made up their minds to establish two forms for naming, *tôn mian ou xreôn estin* – wherein they have gone astray! And they distinguished contrariwise according to the appearance and established signs apart from one another: Here the aetherial Fire of flame, gentle and very light, everywhere the same with itself but not with the other; and then again that other by itself, the opposite, obscure Night – a dense and heavy appearance.

Light and Darkness or Night, the two forms established by mortals, lie at the beginning of the learning process initiated by the goddess, but we should note that what is repeatedly and emphatically accentuated here is the separation of these forms.[6] On the other hand, the passage following the announcement of the "appropriate world-arrangement" (after 8.60-1) strikes a completely different chord:

> Now since everything has been named Light and Night and what corresponds to their powers has been attributed to each thing, everything is full of Light and invisible Night together – both equal, since Nothing partakes in neither (9).

What remains beyond any doubt in this difficult fragment is that both forms henceforth cooperate with one another on an equal standing, in order to determine and dominate the world order. But already the word *diakosmos* implies a "through each another" (*dia-*) of both forms and sets the course for introduc-

---

6 Phrases originating in the military domain, such as "contrariwise" (*antia*), "apart from one another" (*chôris ap' allêlôn*) and "opposite" (*tantia*), are placed at the beginning of these verses. This endows them with additional weight so as to emphasize the resolute separation of Light and Night, which accordingly remain in strict isolation from one another and in mutual exclusion and opposition, as posited by mortals.

ing the concept of *mixture*, first developed by Parmenides and continuously employed in the "appropriate" part of the Doxa.

The decisive restriction of the validity of the term "deceitful" to the opinions (*doxai*) of mortals, as portrayed and criticized in 8.54-9, frees the goddess once and for all from the reproach of common deceit.[7] This restriction would at the same time place *apatêlos* in a close connection with the statement following two lines later, "wherein they have gone astray," so as to open up the possibility for a new understanding of the subordinate relative clause *tôn mian ou xreôn estin*. The illustration of the relationship between both forms in this thorny clause remains not only grammatically highly controversial and unclear in its precise meaning. It is also questionable whether it reproduces a critical position of the goddess or whether it belongs to the criticized system of human conjectures.[8] Now if the former holds true, then it is difficult to identify the human error reproached in the second half of the verse. For what would be erroneous, if the first half of the verse expressed a position of the goddess herself (or, in other words, possessed the mark of the "appropriate" Doxa)?

We therefore conclude that the abruptly formulated clause in 54a denotes and expresses exactly the mistake made by deceptive mortal opinions that will be reproached in the adjacent phrase in 54b and then corrected by the "appropriate" divine Doxa. Mortals posit the forms in a condition of absolute separation, so that in each case "a one (i.e. a unity) of them is not necessary," and their error rests exactly in the incompatibility

---

7 The following positive or "appropriate" Doxa can thus never become part of a Parmenidean "delusion," as Reinhardt (1916: 25-6) and many others have thought.

8 For an overview of the most important interpretations of the present point see Tarán (1965: 217-21). I follow him in the account of the grammar and the translation of 8.53-4, but certainly not in his interpretation of Doxa as wrong altogether and as an illustration of Non-Being.

and the mutual exclusion of both forms.[9] The passage 8.53-9 embodies these erroneous human conjectures, which is why it is called "deceitful" and its fundamental thesis of mutually excluding forms misleading:

> For they made up their minds to establish two forms for naming, a unity of which is not [deemed] necessary [to name] – wherein they have gone astray![10]

---

9 A similar position has been advanced by Gallop (1984: 10-11), who however sees no possibility of preventing the error and calls the cosmology following after 8.60 "false" (1984: 21). Curd (1998: 104-10) also views the "enantiomorphism" of the two forms as the fundamental problem of the Doxa: "It is not plurality itself but opposition that is at the root of the problem" (1998: 110). And she concludes: "If only Light and Night were genuine entities rather than interdefined opposites, Parmenides' cosmology would give an account of the world as experienced [...] that would pass tests based on the fundamental *krisis*, 'is or is not'" (1998: 116). But what Curd presents here in the *modus irrealis* is exactly what we hold to be an adequate description of the appropriate Doxa after 8.60; this Doxa is indeed compatible with the truth of Being and able to pass all "tests," for precisely the reasons mentioned by Curd! – Schwabl has also potentially distinguished between "erroneous opinions of mortals" and a "presentation of a cosmology through the goddess herself" (1968: 399), but without further pursuing this crucial distinction. Other interpretations that bear signs of such a distinction have recently been offered by Graham (1999: 168-9) and Lesher (1999: 240: "a credible cosmology purged of the errors that have infected all previous mortal thinking, one fully consistent with the conception of 'what is' set out in fragments B2 to B8").

10 In offering this translation (proposed also by Tarán 1965: 220), I essentially follow Schwabl (1968: 395), thereby moderating an earlier criticism (Thanassas 1997: 162). My own previous translation ("of which the one should not be," 1997: 166-7) has been rightly criticized by Rechenauer (2001: 228-229). Schwabl was completely correct in his insight that the mistake of mortals lies in their inability to grasp and articulate the unity of Light and Night. But whereas he sees the unity that corrects that error in a Being as "unity of op-

The following "appropriate," divine Doxa, which commences at 8.60 in order to prevent that error, will show that both forms are complementary, each requiring the other.[11] This duality, however, the conjunction (in Kantian terms) of "critique" and "doctrine," means not only that Doxa cannot be false, but also that *the* Doxa does not even exist – except in the exclusively extensional sense that would denote the section of the poem beginning with B 8.50. This section deals with *dokein*, i.e. a human "acceptance," "assumption" or "consideration"[12] that remains oriented to what is given in the phenomena. This mode of human "acceptance," however, is refracted into a number of perspectives, each of which contains different possibilities for analysis and appraisal. In other words, the phrases "deceitful words" and "world-arrangement" (*diakosmos*) denote two dif-

---

posites" (1968: 403) of Light and Night, I would rather point at the unity of the divine *diakosmos*, as a system of mixture of both forms. Schwabl was undoubtedly correct in his analysis that Being plays a role in the Doxa; but the role of Being is not stated there directly and in ontological terms (as Schwabl seems to suggest), but is only indirectly present. Within the perspective of Doxa, the mortals' mistake lies in having overlooked not Being *eo ipso*, but rather the *diakosmos* in the sense of mixture. The goddess does not appeal here to the unity of Being, but to that of the *diakosmos*. If the reverse were the case, then the rest of Doxa, including the appropriate cosmology, would be redundant.

11 Hölscher (1968: 107), on the contrary, sees an endorsement of complementarity already in the position depicted at 8.54a – but then what would be the error? The same critique applies also to Coxon's translation: "of which it is wrong to name only one" (1986: 76). Both Coxon and Hölscher, however, underscore that the crucial innovation of Parmenidean cosmology is its dualism and the complementarity of both forms (although this in my view cannot be detected in 8.55-59, but only after 8.60).

12 Cf. Mourelatos' excellent analysis of the "positive (though defeasible) sense" of the so-called *dok*-words (1970: 194-202).

ferent levels and aims of Doxa. It is important that these levels
and aims not be conflated.

The "decision" to "establish" the forms seems to imply an agent
of this decision, and thus a view of Doxa as doxography or eristic.[13] That "establishing," however, is not so much evidence of
an "original freedom" of the "human spirit," which "constitutes
itself in freedom";[14] it does not denote an intentional action
or a (pre-) historical event, but rather portrays a fundamental
fact and an essential mark of humans as such.[15] The "decision"
of mortals to name both forms is thus *not historically situated*[16]
and is not intended to bolster human freedom, but rather to
show the "posited" character of the system criticized here, as
well as the limitations of its claims. As in 1.31, so again in 8.51
the required "understanding" demands an interpretive penetra-
tion and a translation of a common world representation into
categories invented by Parmenides himself. This initial "understanding" is characterized by a peculiar negativity: it is not an
insight into the features of the world, but instead into a false
epistemological stance. Clearly, it is not only *ontology* (in the
Aletheia section) that originates with Parmenides, but also *epis-
temology* as a critique of knowledge (in the Doxa section).

If Parmenides is dealing neither with a specific earlier philosophical system, nor with a deliberate human construct, but
is rather delineating a model for presenting and comprehend-
ing given human opinions, then precisely which opinions are
presented, discussed, "understood" and rejected? Furthermore,
for what reason, precisely, are Light and Night defined as the

---

13 See also above, p. 19-20.

14 Mansfeld (1964: 215-6).

15 Held (1980: 549).

16 We follow here Hölscher (1968: 112).

pillars of this system? The pair of Light and Night certainly forms a significant and widespread contrast, common in both traditional Greek poetry and everyday understanding.[17] But this contrast occupies a key position in the poem because human knowledge *qua* "assuming" (*dokein*) is founded on sense perception in general and on sight in particular.[18] Light and Night are accordingly thematized at 8.53-9 precisely as conditions of sight and of sensible knowledge. They exclude one another, because everything either reveals itself in the Light as present or withdraws from all (sensible) knowledge into the obscurity of Night. In their, as it were, transcendental function established by the mortals' distinction "according to the appearance" (*demas*), the two forms are by no means equivalent or of equal standing: *Light is here the positive condition of knowledge, whereas darkness inhibits it.*[19]

The relation of the "deceptive" Doxa to the Aletheia is not to be sought in the former's supposed assimilation of (one of) the forms to *eon*,[20] but rather in an *implicit, unreflected and*

17 Cf. Bultmann (1948).

18 The overall preeminence of sight is reflected in the ancient Greek expressions for "knowledge"; cf. Snell (1924).

19 This interpretation can be confirmed through the detailed description of the two forms, but also of the "signs" potentially distinct from them. In contrast to the signs of Being, which "are" (8.2), the signs of both forms are "established" by mortals, and indeed "apart from one another." To Light is attributed the "aetherial fire," which is accompanied by the positive qualities of mildness and lightness, whereas Night is "dense and heavy," but also *adaês*. It is precisely this adjective that unites in the manifold of its meanings the three-fold deficiency of this form: it is both "unknowing" as well as "unrecognized" – both since all light (*daos*) is absent from it.

20 Although Fire in the "deceptive" Doxa is conceived to be "the same with itself (*eôutô tôuton*) but not with the other," whereas Night "by itself" (*kat' auto*) stands opposite to it, it is not the case that signs of Being from fr. 8 are here attributed to the forms. A link between this

thoughtless ontological implication which results from the role
of Night as a source of perceptual ignorance. Whereas humans
hold everything that is standing and presenting itself in the
Light to be knowable, all that is invisible eludes their sight
and knowledge; it is overlooked and covered up, ultimately it
is treated as not-being. Of course, humans do not reflect on
Being and Non-Being as such. Nonetheless, they do follow a
tacit, hidden ontology, wherein Being and Non-Being are *il-
legitimately* represented by Light and Night respectively. The
ontological categories of the crossroads are thus obscured, dis-
figured and deprived of their conceptual precision and sharp-
ness. While mortals are incapable of using *nous* to make the
distinction between Being and Non-Being, they carry out a
separation "according to the appearance," in which they rend
the world apart and create *caesura*. They lapse into a sensualist
fallacy, separating everything into presence and absence and
tending to treat Night as equivalent to Non-Being.[21]

It cannot be ruled out that this Parmenidean model of understanding the deceptive Doxa was influenced by the Pythagorean opposites.[22] Such a relation, however, does not allow for
the rehabilitation of the doxographic-eristic interpretation of
Doxa, nor should it tempt us to see Parmenides as a "dissident

---

passage and Aletheia has rather to be sought in the illustration of the
"third way," where identity and difference occur also in the context
of the "wandering" mortals (cf. 6.8-9 and below, p. 77-9).

21 Hence it is not Parmenides himself, but the erring mortals who asso-
ciate tacitly the one form (Light) with Being, the other (Night) with
Non-Being. A supremacy of Light, and the notion of a "metaphysics
of Light" altogether, is not only irrelevant here, but it illustrates exactly what Parmenides attempts to overcome within his Doxa.

22 "Light" and "dark," for instance, are contained in the "table of opposites" (*Met.* 986a 20 ff.), which is certainly post-Parmenidean but
probably systematizes earlier philosophical views.

Pythagorean"[23] – not to mention the schematic conception, utterly lacking in evidence, of the whole of early Greek philosophy as an ongoing struggle between "Eleatics" and "Pythagoreans." The contrariety of both forms of Light and Night presumably does not stem from the specifically Pythagorean doctrine of "opposites as principles of Being,"[24] but rather from the general tendency of early Greek philosophy to think in oppositions. The two forms in their relation to one another specify and conceptualize the pre-philosophical world-view, whereas their respective signs make a mytho-poetic representation of the dualism possible. Ultimately, Parmenides will decisively transform and overcome the traditional polar contrariety. The subsequent "appropriate" Doxa will abandon the evaluative judgment of the opposites and in particular the priority of Light, in favor of *an equality of both forms* – and this will be only one of the many transformations of traditional motifs effected by Parmenides.

As the tense change from aorist (*katethento*) to perfect (*onomastai*) indicates, the divine, "appropriate" Doxa positively takes up the accomplished human "decision" and the original positing of both forms, while the present tense (*esti*) finally corroborates their status as existing entities:

> Everything is full of Light and invisible Night together –
> both equal, since Nothing partakes in neither (9.3-4).

There is a grammatical indication marking the move from "deceptive" to "appropriate" Doxa. The personal pronoun "I," which in Greek is dispensable, is added here strictly for emphasis, underscoring in a linguistically significant way the revelatory character of what follows:

---

23 So Cornford (1939: 28), similarly Raven (1948: 21, 176, and passim). Coxon (1986: 19) also asserts a Pythagorean influence.

24 See *Met.* 986b 3.

> All this appearing world-arrangement *I* declare to you ap-
> propriately, so that no mortal view may ever outstrip you
> (8.60-1).

The categorical confirmation in 9.4 that Nothing is not to be
found in either form hinders its interference in the cosmic process. Night, which, according to 9.3, is "invisible," *is* just as
much as Light is. This fends off the ontological implications of
the mortal understanding of the Night described above: both
forms are recognized in their cooperation and interpenetration
(*homou, dia-*). This first formulation of the concept of *mixture*
is fundamentally new in contrast to the Milesian assumption
of a single principle and henceforth determines not only the
Parmenidean world-view, but the whole of ensuing cosmology.
Parmenides is not only the father of ontological monism,[25] but
also (in the Doxa section) of cosmological *dualism*.

Both forms no longer function as conditions of erroneous
human conjectures but rather as material components of a
dynamically conceived unity-endowing process.[26] Of crucial importance is here the concept of "power" (*dynamis*), which is
introduced for the forms in 9.2 and makes possible their oper-
ating within the cosmic process. The world's generation is then
described in fr. 12:

> For the narrower [rings] were filled with unmixed Fire and
> those next to them with Night, but a portion of flame is sent
> forth [among them]. And in the middle of them the goddess
> who governs everything; for everywhere she rules over hate-
> ful birth and mixture, sending the female to mingle with
> male and again conversely the male with female.

The sexes here are not conceived as opposites, as in the Pythagorean "table," but rather "mingle" from the beginning

---

25 In the Aletheia, and in the sense stated above, p. 57-9.

26 The exact procedure and method of this transformation, however, is
    not discernible from the preserved fragments.

through divine influence. The same cosmic goddess then (fr. 13) causes unifying Eros to be the "first of all gods devised." In contrast, for example, to Hesiod, who lets Chaos emerge as the first divinity, Parmenides once more presents mixture, here in the figure of Eros, as the most primordial reality. The concept of mixture is then incorporated into the very language of the poem, when, for example, a beautiful verse (fr. 14) calls the moon "night-shining" (*nyktifaes*).

Parmenides' detailed account of the "generation" and the "works" of the world has been but sparsely preserved, and the indirect tradition is seldom clear or consistent.[27] We can assume, however, that the "appropriate" presentation of the goddess ends with fr. 19:

> In this way, according to the opinion, these things were born and now are, and hereafter, having grown up, they will reach their end. For each of them humans established a distinctive name.

What was previously dismissed as irrelevant for Being in the Aletheia section, namely temporality, structures here, with its tripartite order, the narrative of the goddess. Her term "according to the opinion" (*kata doxan*, in the singular) underscores the systematic integration of the prior explanations given one after the other, while at the same time again recalling the limits of these attempts: coming-to-be and passing-away are *only* treated "according to the opinion" and do not merit an ontological rehabilitation. While the concept of generation is useful and even indispensable in the Doxa section, where the goddess deals with particular entities, its inclusion in the Aletheia would be disastrous. Generation would there mean nothing less than the generation of Being itself, which, given the fun-

---

27 The most important contributions to a reconstruction of Parmenidean cosmogony and cosmology have been carried out by Reinhardt (1916: 10-32), Tarán (1965: 231-68), Hölscher (1986: 105-12), Laks (1990), and Bollack (1990).

damental ontological distinction, could only have arisen out of Non-Being.

The concept of mixture ultimately underlies the critique of sense perception developed in 16:

> According each time to the mixture of the much-wandering limbs emerges thought in humans; for [human thought] is the same with what the nature of the limbs thinks, in each and all humans. For [human] thought is [result of] the preponderant.[28]

The reference to the "much-wandering limbs" insinuates that it is "deceptive" opinions that are again thematized here, now with the aim of clarifying their inconsistency and their divergences as effects of the cosmic mixture. The specific mixture of Light and Darkness in each phenomenon is perceived differently by different people because they dispose over different mixtures of "limbs." The resultant "thought" (*noos*) does not seek truth and Being, but rather "occurs" or "emerges" (*parestêken*) for humans as a result of their entanglement in perception and sensibility.

The significance and the consequences of equating both forms become clear, however, from a perspective that we can gain only through the indirect tradition of the testimonies. In one of them, Theophrastus informs us that Parmenides attributed the capacity of sense perception to the dead as well: Whereas the living experience light, warmth and voice, the dead perceive cold and silence (DK28 A46). Simplicius, on his part, reports of the goddess of mixture that she "once sends the souls from the visible into the invisible, and once the other way around" (introductory remark to fr. 13). Here, the two forms and their signs or powers present themselves in the se-

---

28 For the interpretation of this highly disputed fragment, cf. Mansfeld (1964: 187-8). For *to pleon* as "the full" instead of "the preponderant" in the sense of "the more," cf. Tarán (1965: 256-8) and Laks (1990).

ries "Light-life-warmth-voice-visible" and "Night-death-cold-silence-invisible." While these series appear as opposites in the common, erroneous conjectures and implicitly represent Being and Non-Being, Parmenides seeks to demonstrate that the second series likewise belongs to Being. At this point, the fact that both forms *are* (emphasized at 9.4) coincides with Hölscher's recognition of the "existential consequences" of the doctrine of Being: "Death exists no less than life. – There is no dying: that is, for human existence, the doctrine that states in physicalist language: there is neither generation nor corruption."[29]

---

29 Hölscher (1968: 129).

6

ALETHEIA **AND** *DOXA***:**
THE HUMAN AND THE DIVINE

Although fr. 2 calls the two ontological routes the "only" ones, fr. 6 introduces a further path:

> This is necessary to say and to think: Being [*eon*] is; for Being [*einai*] is, whereas Nothing is not. This I bid you to consider. And first <I will convey>[1] you along this first route of inquiry, but then also along that, on which ignorant mortals

---

1 Since the path named at 6.1-2 is obviously the route of Being, the conventional replacement for the missing verb at 6.3 by *eirgô* ("I hold you back," first in Diels 1897: 68, with appeal to a supposed analogy with 7.2) can hardly be tenable. It would have to be a verb with a positive meaning, one that does not promise to "hold back" but rather to lead along the two paths mentioned here: along the first route of Being, and along the "third way" of mortals; cf. also Cordero (1979: 21-4) and Nehamas (1981: 102-6). Although I agree with Cordero and Nehamas in rejecting Diels' *eirgô*, I am not so far convinced by their efforts to determine the missing verb (proposing *arxei* and *arxô* respectively), and I would prefer to withhold my judgment. My own "convey" stresses here the positive force of the missing verb, without indicating a specific supplementation. I see the current situation as a challenge for philologists to submit compelling proposals. – Trying to reject any notion of a third "way," and after rightly stressing that "the presentation of the first way takes place in the whole of 6.1b-2a," Cordero concludes: "*So* the new way that Parmenides presents immediately afterward is the second way. There is no room for a 'third way'" (2004: 98; our emphasis). This argument appears to me as a typical case of begging the question.

> wander, two-headed; for helplessness in the breasts guides
> their confused thought, and they are carried on, deaf and
> blind alike, dazed, hordes without judgment, for whom to
> be and not to be are considered the same and not the same,
> and for everything there is a backward-turning path.

This passage recalls the general acknowledgment of human
ignorance and powerlessness, frequently voiced in Greek epic
and early lyric.[2] This parallel, however, should not obscure the
distinctiveness of Parmenides' critique, which is here formulated exclusively in ontological categories and takes aim only at
the ontological frailty of mortals.

This "third way" does not contradict the assertion of fr. 2
that there are "only" two routes. It is not identified as a "route
of inquiry,"[3] and in fact it is not a genuine route at all, but
rather a presentation of what it is to be ignorant of the "only"
routes of Thinking. In such ontological indecisiveness, Being
and Non-Being are not comprehended as irreconcilable opposites, but are held to be "the same" – when, for instance, everyday speech places them next to each other, or when traditional
cosmologies mix them up with one another. Mortals are called
"two-headed" because they do not keep a clear head, instead allowing themselves to be unthinkingly guided by their "breasts."
Their ontological insufficiency is seen as nescience and makes
them appear as the opposite of the "wise man" from the proemium (*eidôs fôs*, 1.3).

Human beings are *ontologically* "deaf" and "blind," precisely
because they are given over to perception:

> For never shall this prevail, nonbeings to be; but do hold
> back your thought from this route of inquiry. Nor let much-
> experienced habit force you along that other route, to ply an
> aimless eye and noisy ear and tongue, but judge by *logos* the

---

2 Cf. especially Mansfeld (1964: 3-32).

3 Cf. Wiesner (1996: 111).

much-contesting refutation presented by me. Sole the account still remains of the route, that Is (7, 8.1-2a).[4]

While in fr. 6 the third non-route was opposed to the route of
Being, in fr. 7 it is dismissed together with the route of Non-
Being. Fr. 6 criticized the ontological consequences of "wandering," while fr. 7 points out the causes of this errancy: perception and language. Language functions here less as a source
of error than as the "continual support and confirmation"[5] of
the error stemming primarily from the crisis of the senses.

Since the word *aisthêsis* does not occur here, we should not
project onto Parmenides a cohesive concept of "perception."[6]
He nevertheless does seem to possess a specific notion of perception, in contrast to which he clearly defines his concept of true
"thought." Here sensibility is for the first time identified as a
source of error and rejected as *incapable of any cognition whatsoever*. The eye is described as "aimless," because in its many aims
it misses the only one to be sought: Being. Hearing is "noisy,"
because it takes up into language the apparently real mixture
of Being and Non-Being and thoughtlessly reproduces it. The
goddess places the *logos* of her adept under the obligation to
overcome this uncritical "habit"; he is to serve "thought" and to
carry out the "much-contesting" (because "unremittingly necessary"[7]) refutations of the persistent threat of Non-Being.

We can hardly exaggerate the importance of Reinhardt's "discovery" of the "third way" in view of illuminating the structure
of the poem and the argument of the goddess. It would nevertheless be precipitous simply to identify the Doxa section of
the poem with that "third way."[8] Indeed, given the plurality

---

4 Fr. 8 connects immediately to fr. 7.

5 According to Buchheim (1994: 134).

6 Cf. Gadamer (GW 7: 15).

7 Gadamer (GW 7: 27).

8 As Reinhardt, before many others, did: "*doxa* [...] is nothing but the
   third way of inquiry" (1916: 69); transl. in Mourelatos (1974: 303).

of themes and intentions effective in the second part of the poem, the simple, unqualified use of *the* Doxa seems altogether misleading. In view of this, the presentation undertaken above discerned four distinctive perspectives on Doxa:

(1) Understanding the deceptive human conjectures and demonstrating their error (8.53-9).

(2) Presenting an appropriate positive Doxa that rests on a mixture of both forms instead of their separation, thus counteracting the deception (8.60 ff.).

(3) Portraying the genesis of the deceptive opinions, the divergences of which are traced back to differences in the perceptual apparatus (16).

(4) Giving (in the Aletheia) an ontological evaluation and rejecting the deceptive opinions by demonstrating their path to be the "third (non-) way" (6, 7).

These perspectives share the common characteristic that they address phenomenality as such. Their subject matter is the manifold of the world of appearances in the mode of its appearing and in the mode in which we take it up (*dokein*). The four perspectives are not "false," but instead fulfill, each in its own fashion, the task of "learning" and "understanding": they are altogether true.[9]

For a criticism of this view, see Hölscher (1986: 76-7, 103, 109).

9 The contrast between perspectives (1) and (2) can be articulated through the following key concepts:
    "deceitful ordering – appropriate appearing world-arrangement";
    "mortal opinions – I declare to you";
    "gone astray – never outstrip you";
    "a unity is not necessary – Light *and* Night";
    "contrariwise, apart – together";
    "apart from one another – through each other (*dia-*)";

As for the question of how the two parts of the poem are related, it is broached at 1.31-2 and 9.4 and can now be recast as
a question of how truth is related to the four perspectives listed
above. With respect to the deceptive assumptions, their genesis
and ontological evaluation,[10] Reinhardt's answer remains valid:
the goddess "brings truth about the delusion" of mortals[11] and
this truth in no way competes with that of Being, but rather
presupposes it. However, it would be fatal to conclude that the
positive Doxa,[12] which indeed adequately describes the actual
world-arrangement, belongs to that mortal "delusion," or to
comprehend it as a mere "deduction" from the "third way" and
as a "transposing" of the "single fundamental form [Being *and*
Non-Being] into spatial categories."[13]

Certainly, as Reinhardt showed, "the three 'ways of inquiry'
are the natural result of a *single* question."[14] But this unity holds
good solely for the first part, within which the "third way" is
portrayed, and is irrelevant for the positive Doxa *per se*, which
corrects precisely the meaninglessness of the "third way." Ultimately, Reinhardt's core idea that "Non-Being is superadded

---

"[unequal, Night being analogous to Non-Being] – both equal, since
Nothing partakes in neither";

"obscure Night, a dense and heavy appearance – [the invisible Night
is]."

Finally, while in (1) the difference between "Light-life-warmth-voice-
visibility" and "Night-death-cold-silence-invisibility [Hades]" is interpreted as an ontological discrepancy and the second of these series is
regarded as non-being, in (2) the second series acquires an equal ontological validity, belonging to Being. The two series display no ontological distinction!

10 That is perspectives (1), (3), and (4) above.

11 Reinhardt (1916: 25).

12 Perspective (2) above.

13 Reinhardt (1916: 71, 80-1); transl. in Mourelatos (1974: 304, 309-
    10).

14 Reinhardt (1916: 65); transl. in Mourelatos (1974: 299).

to Being and connects itself to it,"[15] thus allowing the world's origination, proves to be extremely non-Parmenidean; for "the force of conviction will never permit that out of Non-Being something arises [i.e. is added] alongside Being" (8.12-3).

In contrast to such interpretive strategies, which remain oriented to the metaphysical model of *derivatio* and which demand the unlikely operation of "deducing" the world of appearances from (onto)logical categories, we can arrive at a more reasonable determination of the relation between Aletheia and positive Doxa, if we take them as two *independent* and *complementary* kinds of inquiry. The Aletheia is directed to the Being of appearances, while the positive Doxa aims at an account of the way in which the appearances appear.[16] These two distinct inquiries intersect at only two points, the two above-mentioned passages (1.31-2 and 9.4), which are, however, of inestimable significance. At 1.31-2, Being is introduced as the Being of what appears (*dokounta*). It is not a "transcendent" object, nor

---

15 Reinhardt (1916: 80); transl. in Mourelatos (1974: 310), with modifications. While Reinhardt conceives Doxa as synthesis and mixture of both ontological paths, others have declared it to be, so to speak, an emanation of Being. Heidegger describes it as "belonging to Being" (1935: 120), and a similar stand has been taken by Beaufret (1955: 48) and Fink (1985: 191), partly also by Gadamer (GW 6: 19) and Hölscher (1986: 121); Schwabl (1956: 148) and Finkelberg (1999: 235) have also called Doxa the "continuation" of the first route. The spectrum of interpretations has been completed by Tarán, who completely denies the existence of a "third way" (1965: 208) and identifies the Doxa section as the route of Non-Being (1965: 229-30); similar interpretations have been offered by Cordero (1979: 12-21; 2004: 138-143) and Nehamas (1981: 105-6).

16 As one of the few interpreters who respect the fact that Doxa contains "Parmenides' own philosophy of nature," Steiger presents the duality of Aletheia and Doxa as a manifestation of an intrinsic *aporia*, or as a feature of philosophy itself (1986: 203). But I think that Steiger exaggerates when he views this duality as an instance of "incompatibility" or "contradiction."

a world-negating hypostasis, but can only be thought and experienced along with the world of appearances. Parmenides, accordingly, is not peddling a "two-world-theory," but presents the one world in the light of two different ways of knowing it. The "noetic" kind of knowledge discovers Being everywhere, whereas the "doxastic" corrects the errors in the world-view of mortals and provides a definitive presentation of the appearing world. This presentation, in turn, only attains "appropriateness" because in it Non-Being has disappeared and everything is "full" of the forms of Light and Night (9.3), which both belong to the realm of Being. The forms are now cleared of the presence of Nothingness. They serve Being's cosmological epiphany.

The emphasis on the absence of Non-Being in the divine Doxa (9.4) supports the hypothesis that the truth previously grasped provides also constitutive moments of *an appropriate Doxa*. We must understand this not in the sense that it allows for a "creation" or "deduction" of "earth and sun and moon and aether," but rather that it provides a criterion for the tenability and a guarantee of the unsurpassability of this divine world-arrangement.[17] Reinhardt's explicit demand for a "mediation" between Aletheia and (positive) Doxa thus needs to be radicalized in one respect, restricted in another. The radicalization would mean that *both parts of the poem have as their theme one and the same object*, namely the Cosmos, the world of phenomena, which is grasped in the Doxa *as appearing*, in the Aletheia *as being*. On the other side, the truth of Being and the appropriate Doxa would emerge as two kinds of knowledge that exhibit points of contact and prove to be compatible, but nonetheless

---

17 In this respect we agree with Curd's thesis that "the problem and deception lie, apparently, not in the attempt to give a cosmological account, but in the ontological failings of this cosmology" (1998: 110). But this holds true only for the erroneous Doxa presented in 8.53-59.

retain their irreducibility and complementarity – both as distinct steps of Parmenides' dual strategy of "saving the phenomena."

In view of a more precise account of this dual structure, it is important not to overlook the fact that in the context of Doxa "humans" and "mortals" are recurrently mentioned (nine times in the preserved fragments), while the truth of Being is presented as an eminently divine insight that radically challenges everything human.[18] Of course, even appropriate Doxa is a divine gift, but it does justice to the human world-view by defining and distinguishing itself with respect to the other "mortal views" (8.61). All four Doxa-perspectives are ultimately tied to the *conditio humana*, which is itself essentially shaped by phenomenality. Ontology, on the other hand, oversteps these limits and can be conveyed only from a place "far from the step of humans" (1.27), beyond the "gates of Night and Day" (1.11). If Aletheia and (positive) Doxa are presented as parallel to the divine and the human respectively, then we have a further reason why their difference cannot be waived: The gulf that separates them is as wide as the one dividing the human from the divine.

Parmenides meets the goddess of truth at the end of a journey described in the proemium. Let us briefly return to its presentation. The poet's chariot is drawn by "sagacious horses" along the "road of the goddess" – "as far as [his] impulse might reach." This vigorous impulse marks perhaps the very first manifestation of a philosophical Self and of thought's spontaneity, although the poet does not determine the direction or destination of the ride. These are initially controlled by the horses, then by the daughters of the Sun. Against the view that the course leads "towards the light" and thus features a "metaphor-

---

18 For an interesting assessment of this duality, cf. Bodnár (1989).

ic of light," it has been objected that the maidens' movement from "the House of Night towards the light" has taken place *before* their encounter with the poet and does not extend to the common journey presently described.[19]

The journey thus takes place in a topography left vague and uncertain, probably intentionally. As for the minute, almost surreal description of certain details of the journey, it serves to underscore how extraordinary this journey has been. Parmenides here borrows from traditional motifs such as the journeys of Odysseus or Phaethon,[20] and especially from Hesiod's description of *chaos* and of the "house of Night" located in it, whose gate is passed in turn by Day and Night. But Parmenides departs from Hesiod at a decisive juncture.[21] His gateway does not open into a realm "even abhorred by gods,"[22] beyond all order and orientation, but leads to a goddess who warmly welcomes the poet and focuses his complete attention on her speech. In Hesiod's depiction, the gate marks as it were the limits of reason, while the gate in Parmenides functions as *the source and origin of ontology and of philosophical reason altogether.*

The proemium's journey is neither an anabasis anticipating the Platonic *Phaedrus*, nor a katabasis reproducing Pythagorean mystical motifs. The journey surpasses the cosmic horizon, it moves beyond the point of encounter between Day and Night, bypassing the "aetherial gates" erected upon a "stone threshold" embracing heaven and earth,[23] and leads to a place "far from the step of humans." It does not testify to a "genuine religious

---

19 Burkert (1969: 7-9) For a detailed discussion of the proemium, see Bowra (1937), Jaeger, (1947: 90-8), Fränkel (1955: 1-14).

20 Cf. Havelock (1958). The full extent of the thematic and stylistic influence of the *Odyssey* on the poem has been shown in an exhaustive manner by Mourelatos (esp. 1970: 12-34).

21 Buchheim (1994: 107) even speaks of a "parody."

22 *Theog.* 739.

23 Burkert (1969: 12).

experience"[24] of a poet "in ecstasy,"[25] neither does it function
as allegorical cloaking.[26] Rather, it "speaks for itself and is to
be understood by itself"[27] – like all poetry. Philosophically relevant in this poetic prelude is the *speed* of the journey to philosophy coupled with the *remoteness and inapproachability* of the
philosophical region, and above all the very fact of portraying
the way to philosophy as the "way of a goddess" and of adopting
her as the author of this innovative ontological truth.

Laying emphasis on the verb "to carry" (*pherein*), which occurs four times in the first four lines of the poem, the sup-
posedly motion-denying Parmenides begins a tale that, in its
depiction of the "whirling wheels" and "glowing axle" (1.6-8),
underlines the danger of the journey and its breakneck speed.
Concerning a journey that is otherwise but vaguely described,
Parmenides focuses on several details that emphasize the ex-
treme strain of the cart and the poet's desire for rapid progress.
The journey's outcome is in no way guaranteed. It could abort
at any time, and is in fact interrupted when the poet arrives at
the "gates of Night and Day" (1.11). The realm behind these
gates is guarded by the "much-avenging" goddess of justice
(*Dike*), who nonetheless leaves Parmenides safe and sound and
is coaxed by the maidens "with gentle words" to let them enter.
The detailed presentation of the opening of the gates calls further attention to the resistance and the obstacles that the poet
must overcome, before gaining access to the remote domain
of the anonymous goddess of truth. She first greets him and
assures him that his journey is not due to an "ill fate," but to
"right and justice," and she then promises him an insight into
all possible knowledge. No further elements of action are men-

---

24 This is Jaeger's view (1947: 96), who also speaks of "Parmenides'
   mystery of Being" (1947: 107).

25 Fränkel (1975: 366).

26 See Sextus, *Adv. math.* VII.111 ff. (introduction to fr. 1).

27 Hölscher (1986: 71).

tioned after the monologue of the goddess begins. She herself is free of all traditionally divine characteristics. Her presence indicates simply –albeit emphatically– the inclusion of the divine as such in the way to philosophy.

The device of presenting the entire poem from 1.24 on as the speech of a goddess is poetically unique. Her role evokes comparison with that Muse whom the poet calls upon at the beginning of the Homeric epics as the source of his narrative. Assigning certain, true and indubitable knowledge to the gods had had a long tradition,[28] but led to divergent attitudes. Whereas Hesiod,[29] for instance, appealed to the divine authority of the Muses and presented himself as inspired by them in a thoroughly "honest" and true poetical narrative, Xenophanes preferred a skeptical stance that denied human beings any possibility of reliable knowledge. Parmenides, in contrast, asserts both the *divinity* and the *attainability* of true knowledge. The chosen poet is indeed apprised of the truth, and he can carry out his vague "impulse," even if this is only possible by becoming the "consort" (1.24) of divine charioteers and by "arriving" at the house of this goddess (1.25). But the divine nature of true knowledge here takes a completely novel turn, and the meaning of Parmenides' calling upon a divine entity goes far beyond the merely extrinsic authorization of the poem. Recourse to the goddess might seem like a step backwards compared to the philosophers who were already articulating their theories in their own names. But this is not a relapse into a long obsolete, naïve, archaic stance, but rather a conscious and intentional employment of revelation as "the natural surface cover for this most radical of all philosophies."[30]

The question of the relation between Aletheia and Doxa reveals what is perhaps its most interesting aspect when it is posed

---

28 See on this point Snell (1953: 136-47).

29 *Theog.* 27-8.

30 Reinhardt (1916: 67); transl. in Mourelatos (1974: 301).

as the question of the *transition* from "all too human" Doxa to
the Aletheia – that is, as a question of the disengagement of
humans from their conditioned existence, and of their attain-
ing the truth of Being at the end of a journey that extends "far
from the step of humans." In this context, the encounter with
the goddess proves to be neither an authentic "experience," nor
an antiquated artifice designed to bestow credibility upon the
philosophy of Being. Rather, that encounter posits the question of the origin of philosophy. Since Parmenides, the self-de-
scription of philosophy as a divine gift has become somewhat
canonical. This account, however, does *not* answer the question
of philosophy's origin, but states explicitly that this question is
one that can only be "answered" in the language of myth.

In his orchestration of the wondrous journey and the encounter with the goddess, Parmenides not only succeeds in integrat-
ing the mythical element into the sphere of philosophy, but
also in showing its limits. The path to the philosophy of Being
can only be "grounded" by a mythical goddess, and this means
that philosophy cannot give an account of its own origin by
means of concepts. The Parmenidean *dea ex machine*, used here
as the midwife of ontology, contributes nothing to the content
of truth. She does not turn Parmenides' poem into a "revealed
philosophy" and does not place it under the dominion of "mys-
ticism." Divine presence is crucial and indispensable only as a
sign of the impossibility of achieving conceptual mastery of
the path that leads to philosophy. It is a mark of philosophy's
groundlessness.

APPENDIX

TRANSLATION OF THE FRAGMENTS

The aim of the following translation is to facilitate an uninterrupted reading of the fragments and to indicate the textual basis of the interpretation presented above. The footnotes point out the major divergences of our reading ("Th") with respect to the two "standard" editions of Diels/Kranz ("DK") and Tarán (1965; here symbolized by "T"). Since fr. 18 has been transmitted only in a Latin translation, it cannot be included in the original fragments and is thus omitted here.

FRAGMENT I

The mares that carry me as far as my impulse might reach
were escorting me, when guiding they placed me on the resounding road
of the goddess,[1] which alone[2] carries everywhere the wise man.
On it I was being carried; for thereon the sagacious horses were carrying me
5 straining the chariot, and maidens were leading the way.
And the axle in the naves was sending forth a pipe's whistle,
glowing; for it was urged on by two whirling
wheels at either end, whenever the daughters of the Sun
hastened to escort [me], having left the House of Night
10 towards the light, having pushed back with their hands their heads' veils.
There stand the gates of the paths of Night and Day,
framed by a lintel and a stone threshold;
they are aetherial, filled with huge wing-doors,
to which the much-avenging Justice holds matching keys.
15 Coaxing her with gentle words, the maidens
skillfully persuaded her to swiftly lift for them
the bolted bar from the gates. And these, opening wide,
created a gaping chasm by swinging in turn
the brazen posts of the wing-doors in their sockets,
20 fitted with bolts and rivets. Straight through them
did the maidens drive the chariot and horses along the broad way.

---

1 T, Th: *daimonos*; DK: *daimones*

2 Th: *kata pant' a<u>tê* [cf. Diels (1897: 48-9)]; DK, T: *kata pant' a<s>tê*

And the goddess received me graciously, took my right hand
in hers, and spoke and thus addressed me:
O young man, consort of immortal charioteers,
25 arriving at our house with the horses that carry you,
welcome! For it was no ill fate that sent you to take
this route, which lies indeed far from the step of humans,
but right and justice. It is necessary that you learn everything:
both the unshaken heart of persuasive[3] truth
30 as well as the mortals' opinions, in which there is no true conviction.
But nevertheless these you shall learn as well, how appearing things
should be accepted: all of them altogether as beings.[4]

FRAGMENT 2

Come now, I shall tell you, and do preserve the account as you heard it,
what are the only routes of inquiry for thinking:
The one, [to think] that Is and that it is impossible not-to-be,
this is the path of persuasion, for it follows upon truth.
5 The other, [to think] that Is-not and that it is necessary not-to-be,
this I tell you is a path without any tidings;
for neither could you know Non-Being –for this is impossible –
nor could you express it.

FRAGMENT 3

… for Thinking and Being are the same

---

3 Th: *eupeitheos*; DK, T: *eukukleos*

4 Th: *per onta*; DK, T: *perônta*

FRAGMENT 4

But see through the thought how absent beings are firmly present to it;
for [thought] will not cut off being from holding fast to being,
as this disperses itself in every way everywhere in order
or as it gathers itself together.

FRAGMENT 5

It is all one to me
where I am to begin; for there I shall return again.

FRAGMENT 6

This is necessary to say and to think: Being is; for Being is,
whereas Nothing is not. This I bid you to consider.
And first <I will convey>[5] you along this first route of inquiry,
but then also along that, on which ignorant mortals
5   wander, two-headed; for helplessness in the
breasts guides their confused thought, and they are carried on,
deaf and blind alike, dazed, hordes without judgment,
for whom to be and not to be are considered the same
and not the same, and for everything there is a backward-turning path.

---

5 [Cf. p. 77, n. 1 above.]

FRAGMENTS 7, 8

For never shall this prevail, nonbeings to be;
but do hold back your thought from this route of inquiry.
Nor let much-experienced habit force you along that other route,
to ply an aimless eye and noisy ear
5   and tongue, but judge by *logos* the much-contesting refutation
1   presented by me.
                    Sole the account still remains
of the route, that Is. And on this route there are signs
very many: that Being [a] is ungenerated and imperishable,
[b] whole and unique, [c] unshaken and [d] complete.[6]

5   [a] Nor was it before, nor will it be, since it is now all together,
one, continuous. For what birth could you seek for it?
How and whence did it grow? From Non-Being I shall not allow you
to say or to think [that it was born], for it is impossible to say or to think
that Is-not; what necessity would have impelled it
10 later or sooner to take its birth from Nothing?
Thus it is necessary either to be completely or not at all.
Nor will the force of conviction ever permit that out of Non-Being[7]
something arises [i.e. is added] alongside Being. Therefore Justice has not
    allowed it
to come to be nor to perish by loosening the fetters,
15 but holds firm. And the decision about these matters lies in this:
either Is or Is-not. Now it has been decided, just as is necessary,
to abandon one route as unthinkable and nameless, for it is not
true, while the other route –that Is– is true.
How could Being perish later on?[8] How could it come to be?
20 For if it came to be, it is not, nor if it is going to be in the future.
Thus coming-to-be is extinguished and perishing is unheard of.

------

6   T, Th: *êde teleston*; DK: *êd' ateleston* [cf. Tarán (1965: 93-5)]

7   DK, Th: *ek mê eontos*; T: *ek tou eontos*

8   DK, Th: *epeit' apoloito*; T: *epeita peloi to*

[b] Nor is it divisible, since it is all alike;

nor is it somewhat more here, which would prevent it from holding
   together,

and somewhat less there, but everything is full of Being.

25 Therefore everything is continuous: Being consorts with Being.

[c] And so, unmovable within the limits of great bonds,

it is without beginning or end, since coming-to-be and perishing

have been banished far away: true conviction has thrust them out.

The same and remaining in the same, it lies by itself

30 and so will remain there firm; for strong necessity

holds it within the bonds of the limit which fences it about.

32 [d] Wherefore it is not right for Being to be incomplete;

33 for it is not in need: if it were, it would lack everything.

42 But since there is an outermost limit, it is completed

from every side, like the body of a well-rounded sphere,

equally strong everywhere from the centre – for it may not

be more or less, here or there.

For neither is there Non-Being to prevent it from reaching

its like, nor is Being such that it might be here more

and there less than Being, since it is all inviolate.

49 Equal thus to itself from everywhere, it uniformly lies within its limits.

34 Thinking and [Being as] the cause of thought are the same;

for without Being, to which it stands committed,

you will not find Thinking. And no necessity[9] is or will be

apart from Being, since Fate has fettered it

to be whole and unmovable. With respect to this have been spoken all
   names[10]

---

9   Th: *ouden chreos estin ê estai*; DK, T: *ouden gar ê estin ê estai*

10 Th: *tô pant' onomastai*; DK, T: *tô pant' onom(a) estai*

that mortals have established, confident that they are true:
coming-to-be and perishing, to be *and* not to be,
41 shift of place and exchange of bright color.

50 Here I end for you my convincing account and thought
about truth. From here onwards learn mortal opinions,
listening to the deceitful ordering of my words.
For they made up their minds to establish two forms for naming,
a unity of which is not [deemed] necessary [to name] – wherein they have
    gone astray!
55 And they distinguished contrariwise according to the appearance and
    established signs
apart from one another: Here the aetherial Fire of flame,
gentle and very light, everywhere the same with itself
but not with the other; and then again that other by itself,
the opposite, obscure Night – a dense and heavy appearance.

60 All this appearing world-arrangement I declare to you appropriately,
so that no mortal view may ever outstrip you.

FRAGMENT 9

Now since everything has been named Light and Night
and what corresponds to their powers has been attributed to each thing,
everything is full of Light and invisible Night together
– both equal, since Nothing partakes in neither.

FRAGMENT 10

You shall know the generation of aether and all aetherial
signs and the destructive works of the splendid sun's
pure torch, and whence they came to be.
And you shall learn the wandering works of the round-faced moon
5 and her generation, and you shall also know the surrounding heaven,
whence it was born and how necessity led and fettered it
to hold the limits of the stars.

FRAGMENT 11

    How earth and sun and moon
and the common aether and the heavenly galaxy and Olympus
the outermost and the hot power of the stars strove eagerly
to come to be.

FRAGMENT 12

For the narrower [rings] were filled with unmixed Fire
and those next to them with Night, but a portion of flame is sent forth
    [among them].
And in the middle of them the goddess who governs everything;
for everywhere she rules over hateful birth and mixture,
5 sending the female to mingle with male and again conversely
the male with female.

FRAGMENT 13

first of all gods she devised Eros…

FRAGMENT 14

night-shining, wandering around the earth, an alien light…

FRAGMENT 15

always looking towards the rays of the sun…

FRAGMENT 16

According each time[1] to the mixture of the much-wandering limbs
emerges thought in humans; for [human thought] is the same
with what the nature of the limbs thinks,
in each and all humans. For [human] thought is [result of] the
    preponderant.

FRAGMENT 17

On the right side boys, on the left girls…

FRAGMENT 19

In this way, according to the opinion, these things were born and now are,
and hereafter, having grown up, they will reach their end.
For each of them humans established a distinctive name.

---

1 T, Th: *hekastot*; DK: *hekastos*.

SELECTED BIBLIOGRAPHY[*]

Allen, R. E. / Furley, D. J. (1975, eds.): *Studies in Presocratic Philosophy*, vol. II: *The Eleatics and the Pluralists*. London: Routledge.

Allen, R. E. (1983, ed.): *Plato's Parmenides. Translation and Analysis*. Oxford: Blackwell.

Aubenque, P. (1987, ed.): *Études sur Parménide* (2 vols.). Paris: J. Vrin.

Austin, S. (1986): *Parmenides: Being, Bounds, and Logic*. New Haven: Yale University Press.

Barnes, J. (1982): *The Presocratic Philosophers*. London: Routledge.

Beaufret, J. (1955): *Parménide. Le poème*. Paris: PUF [4]1991.

Bicknell, P. J. (1968): "Parmenides, Fragment 10." *Hermes* 96, 629-31.

Bodnár, I. M. (1989): "Reason and revelation in Parmenides." *Doxa* 17, 61-67.

Boeder, H. (1962): *Grund und Gegenwart als Frageziel der frühgriechischen Philosophie*. Den Haag: M. Nijhoff.

Boeder, H. (1994): *Das Bauzeug der Geschichte. Aufsätze und Vorträge zur griechischen und mittelalterlichen Philosophie*. Würzburg: Königshausen & Neumann.

Bollack, J. (1990): "La cosmologie parménidéenne de Parménide." In R. Brague / J.-F. Courtine (eds.): *Herméneutique et Ontologie* (Mélanges en hommage à Pierre Aubenque). Paris: Presses Universitaires de France, 17-53.

Bollack, J. (2006): *Parménide, de l'étant au monde*. Lagrasse: Verdier.

---

[*] For a more extensive bibliographical list, see Hermann (2004).

Bormann, K. (1971): *Parmenides. Untersuchungen zu den Fragmenten.* Hamburg: Meiner.

Bowra, C. M. (1937): "The Proem of Parmenides." *Classical Philology* 32, 97-112.

Buchheim, T. (1994): *Die Vorsokratiker. Ein philosophisches Porträt.* München: Beck.

Bultmann, R. (1948): "Zur Geschichte der Lichtsymbolik im Altertum." *Philologus* 97, 1-36.

Burkert, W. (1969): "Das Proömium des Parmenides und die Katabasis des Pythagoras." *Phronesis* 14, 1-30.

Calogero, G. (1932): *Studien über den Eleatismus.* Darmstadt: Wissenschaftliche Buchgesellschaft 1970 [original edition: *Studi sull'eleatismo.* Rom 1932].

Caston, V. / Graham, D. W. (2002, eds.): *Presocratic Philosophy. Essays in Honour of Alexander Mourelatos.* Aldershot/Burlington: Ashgate.

Cordero, N.-L. (1979): "Les deux chemins de Parménide dans les fragments 6 et 7." *Phronesis* 24, 1-32.

Cordero, N.-L. (2004): *By Being, It Is. The Thesis of Parmenides.* Las Vegas: Parmenides Publishing.

Cornford, F. M. (1939): *Plato and Parmenides.* London: Routledge ³1951.

Coxon, A. H. (1986): *The Fragments of Parmenides.* Assen: Van Gorcum.

Curd, P. (1998): *The legacy of Parmenides. Eleatic monism and later presocratic thought.* Princeton: Princeton University Press.

Deichgräber, K. (1958): *Parmenides' Auffahrt zur Göttin des Rechts. Untersuchungen zum Prooimion seines Lehrgedichts.* Mainz/Wiesbaden: Akad. der Wiss. und der Literatur.

Diels, H. (1897): *Parmenides, Lehrgedicht.* Sankt Augustin: Academia ²2003.

Dilcher, R. (2006): "Parmenides on the Place of Mind." In R. King (ed.): *Common to Body and Soul.* Berlin/New York: De Gruyter: 31-48.

Ebert, T. (1989): "Wo beginnt der Weg der Doxa? Eine Textumstellung im Fragment 8 des Parmenides." *Phronesis* 34, 121-38.

Fink, E. (1985): *Grundfragen der antiken Philosophie*. Würzburg: Königshausen & Neumann.

Finkelberg, A. (1999): "Being, Truth and Opinion in Parmenides." *Archiv für Geschichte der Philosophie* 81, 233-48.

Fleischer, M. (2001): *Anfänge europäischen Philosophierens*. Würzburg: Königshausen & Neumann.

Fränkel, H. (1955): "Studies in Parmenides." In Allen/Furley (1975: 1-47).

Fränkel, H. (1975): *Early Greek Poetry and Philosophy*. Oxford: Blackwell.

Fritz, K. von (1945): "*Nous, Noein*, and their Derivatives in Pre-Socratic Philosophy." In Mourelatos (1974: 23-95) [first publication in *Classical Philology* 40 (1945), 223-42, and 41 (1946), 12-34].

Furth, M. (1968): "Elements of eleatic ontology." In Mourelatos (1974: 241-70) [first publication in *Journal of the History of Philosophy* 6, 111-32].

Gadamer, H.-G. (GW): *Gesammelte Werke*. Tübingen: J. C. B. Mohr (Paul Siebeck) 1986-95.

Gadamer, H.-G. (1968, ed.): *Um die Begriffswelt der Vorsokratiker*. Darmstadt: Wissenschaftliche Buchgesellschaft.

Gallop, D. (1984): *Parmenides of Elea, Fragments, A Text and Translation with an Introduction*. Toronto: University of Toronto Press.

Giancola, D. M. (2001): "Toward a Radical Reinterpretation of Parmenides' B3." *Journal of Philosophical Research* 26, 635-653.

Graham, D. W. (1999): "Empedocles and Anaxagoras: Responses to Parmenides." In Long (1999: 159-80).

Graham, D. W. (2002): "Heraclitus and Parmenides." In Caston/Graham (2002: 27-44).

Guthrie, W. K. C. (1965): *A History of Greek Philosophy*, vol. II. Cambridge: Cambridge University Press.

Havelock, E. A. (1958): "Parmenides and Odysseus." *Harvard Studies in Classical Philology* 63, 133-43.

Heidegger, M. (1935): *Einführung in die Metaphysik. Gesamtasugabe*, vol. 40. Frankfurt: Klostermann 1983.

Heidegger, M. (1954): *Was heisst Denken?* Tübingen: Niemeyer.

Heidegger, M. (1957): *Identität und Differenz*. Pfullingen: Neske.

Heinimann, F. (1945): *Nomos und Physis*. Darmstadt: Wissenschaftliche Buchgesellschaft ⁵1987.

Heitsch, E. (1974): *Parmenides. Die Fragmente*. München/Zürich: Artemis ²1991.

Held, K. (1980): *Heraklit, Parmenides und der Anfang von Philosophie und Wissenschaft*. Berlin/New York: de Gruyter.

Hermann, A. (2004): *To Think like God*. Las Vegas: Parmenides Publications.

Hölscher, U. (1968): *Anfängliches Fragen. Studien zur frühgriechischen Philosophie*. Göttingen: Vandenhoeck & Ruprecht.

Hölscher, U. (1976): *Der Sinn von Sein in der älteren griechischen Philosophie*. Heidelberg: Winter.

Hölscher, U. (1986): *Parmenides. Vom Wesen des Seienden*. Frankfurt: Suhrkamp ²1986.

Jaeger, W. (1947): *The Theology of the Early Greek Philosophers*. Oxford: Clarendon Press.

Kahn, C. H. (1969): "The Thesis of Parmenides." *The Review of Metaphysics* 22, 700-24.

Kahn, C. H. (1973): *The Verb "Be" in Ancient Greek*. Boston: Reidel.

Kahn, C. H. (1986): "Retrospect on the Verb 'To Be' and the Concept of Being." In S. Knuuttila / J. Hintikka (eds.): *The Logic of Being*. Dordrecht: Reidel, 1-28.

Kahn, C. H. (1988): "Being in Parmenides and Plato." *La Parola del Passato* 43, 237-61.

Kirk, G. S. / Raven, J. E. (1957): *The Presocratic Philosophers.* Cambridge: Cambridge University Press.

Kirk, G. S. / Stokes, M. C. (1960): "Parmenides' Refutation of Motion." *Phronesis* 5, 1-4.

Laks, A. (1990): "'The More' and 'The Full': On the Reconstruction of Parmenides' Theory of Sensation in Theophrastus, *De Sesnisbus* 3-4." *Oxford Studies in Ancient Philosophy* 8, 1-18.

Lesher, J. H. (1984): "Parmenides' Critique of Thinking. The *polydêris elenchos* of Fragment 7." *Oxford Studies in Ancient Philosophy* 2, 1-30.

Lesher, J. H. (1999): "Early Interest in Knowledge." In Long (1999: 225-49).

Long, A. A. (1963): "The Principles of Parmenides' Cosmogony." *Phronesis* 8, 90-107 [repr. in Allen/Furley (1975: 82-101)].

Long, A. A. (1999, ed.): *The Cambridge Companion to Early Greek Philosophy.* Cambridge: Cambridge University Press.

Long, A. A. (2005): "Parmenides on Thinking Being." In Rechenauer (2005: 227-51).

Manchester, P. B. (1979): "Parmenides and the Need for Eternity." *The Monist* 62, 81-106.

Mansfeld, J. (1964): *Die Offenbarung des Parmenides und die menschliche Welt.* Assen: Van Gorcum.

Mansion, A. (1945): *Introduction à la Physique aristotélicienne.* Louvain: Peeters (2nd ed.).

McKirahan, R. (1994): *Philosophy Before Socrates.* Indianapolis: Hackett.

Mourelatos, A. P. D. (1969): "Comments on 'The Thesis of Parmenides' [= Kahn 1969]." *The Review of Metaphysics* 22, 735-44.

Mourelatos, A. P. D. (1970): *The Route of Parmenides. A Study of Word, Image and Argument in the Fragments.* New Haven: Yale University Press.

Mourelatos, A. P. D. (1973): "Heraclitus, Parmenides, and the Naive Metaphysics of Things." In E. N. Lee et al. (eds.): *Exegesis and Argument: Studies in Greek Philosophy Presented to Gr. Vlastos* (= *Phronesis*, Suppl. Vol. 1). Assen: Van Gorcum, 16-48.

Mourelatos, A. P. D. (1974, ed.): *The Pre-Socratics. A Collection of Critical Essays.* New York: Anchor [Princeton: Princeton University Press ²1993].

Mourelatos, A. P. D. (1976): "Determinacy and Indeterminacy, Being and Non-Being in the Fragments of Parmenides." *Canadian Journal of Philosophy* (Suppl. Vol. 2), 45-60.

Mourelatos, A. P. D. (1979): "Some Alternatives in Interpreting Parmenides." *The Monist* 62, 3-14.

Mourelatos, A. P. D. (1999): "Parmenides and the Pluralists." *Apeiron: A Journal for Ancient Philosophy and Science* 32, 117-29.

Nehamas, A. (1981): "On Parmenides' Three Ways of Inquiry." *Deucalion* (Athens) 33/34, 97-111.

Nehamas, A. (2002): "Parmenidean Being / Heraclitean Fire." In Caston/Graham (2002: 45-64).

Owen, G. E. L. (1960): "Eleatic Questions." *Classical Quarterly* 10, 84-102 [rev. and repr. in Allen/Furley (1975: 48-81)].

Owen, G. E. L. (1966): "Plato and Parmenides on the Timeless Present." *The Monist* 50 (1966), 317-40 [rev. and repr. in Mourelatos (1974: 271-92)].

Owens, J. (1974): "The Physical World of Parmenides." In J. R. O'Donnell (ed.): *Essays in Honour of A. C. Pegis.* Leyden: Brill, 378-95.

Popper, K. (1998): *The World of Parmenides: Essays on the Presocratic Enlightenment.* London: Routledge.

Rapp, C. (2005): "Eleatischer Monismus." In Rechenauer (2005: 290-315).

Raven, J. E. (1948): *Pythagoreans and Eleatics.* Amsterdam: Hakkert ²1966.

Rechenauer, G. (2001): "Neuere Literatur zu den Vorsokrati-
kern." *Philosophische Rundschau* 48, 208-230.

Rechenauer, G. (2005, ed.): *Frühgriechisches Denken*. Göttingen: Vandenhoeck & Ruprecht.

Reinhardt, K. (1916): *Parmenides und die Geschichte der griechischen Philosophie*. Frankfurt: Klostermann ⁴1985 [partly
translated in Mourelatos (1974: 293-311)].

Rijk, L. M. de (1983): "Did Parmenides reject the sensible
world?" In L. P. Person (ed.): *Graceful Reason. Essays in Ancient and Medieval Philosophy Presented to Joseph Owens*. Toronto: Pontifical Institute of Medieval Studies, 29-53.

Robbiano, C. (2006): *Becoming Being. On Parmenides' Trans-
formative Philosophy*. Sankt Augustin: Academia.

Schadewaldt, W. (1978): *Die Anfänge der Philosophie bei den
Griechen*. Frankfurt: Suhrkamp.

Schofield, M. (1970): "Did Parmenides discover Eternity?" *Archiv für Geschichte der Philosophie* 52, 113-35.

Schwabl, H. (1956): "Forschungsbericht" zu Parmenides. *An-
zeiger für die Altertumswissenschaft* 9, 129-56.

Schwabl, H. (1968): "Sein und Doxa bei Parmenides." In Gadamer (1968: 391-422) [first publ. in *Wiener Studien* 66
(1953), 50-75].

Scuto, G. (2005): *Parmenides' Weg. Vom Wahr-Scheinenden zum
Wahr-Seienden*. Sankt Augustin: Academia.

Sedley, D. (1999): "Parmenides and Melissus." In Long (1999:
113-33).

Shorey, P. (1900): Review of A. Patin, *Parmenides im Kampfe ge-
gen Heraklit* (Leipzig: Teubner 1899). *The American Journal
of Philology* 21, 200-16.

Snell, B. (1924): *Die Ausdrücke für den Begriff des Wissens in der
vorplatonischen Philosophie*. Berlin: Weidmannsche Buch-
handlung.

Snell, B. (1953): *The Discovery of the Mind. The Greek Origins
of European Thought*. Oxford: Blackwell.

Steiger, K. (1986): "Die Kosmologie des Parmenides und Empedokles." *Oikumene* 5, 173–236.

Stokes, M. C. (1971): *One and Many in Presocratic Philosophy.* Washington, D.C.: Center for Hellenic Studies.

Tarán, L. (1965): *Parmenides. A Text with Translation, Commentary, and Crtical Essays.* Princeton: Princeton University Press.

Tarán, L. (1979): "Perpetual Duration and Atemporal Eternity in Parmenides and Plato." *The Monist* 62, 43-53.

Thanassas, P. (1997): *Die erste "zweite Fahrt." Sein des Seienden und Erscheinen der Welt bei Parmenides.* Munich: Wilhelm Fink.

Thanassas, P. (2005): "Doxa revisitata." In Rechenauer (2005: 270-89).

Thanassas, P. (2006): "How Many *Doxai* Are There in Parmenides?" *Rhizai* 3, 199-218.

Theunissen, M. (1991): "Die Zeitvergessenheit der Metaphysik. Zum Streit um Parmenides, Fr. 8.5-6a." In: *Negative Theologie der Zeit.* Frankfurt: Suhrkamp, 89-130.

Tugendhat, E. (1970): "Das Sein und das Nichts." In: *Philosophische Aufsätze.* Frankfurt: Suhrkamp 1992, 36-66.

Verdenius, W. J. (1942): *Parmenides. Some Comments on his Poem.* Amsterdam: Hakkert ²1964.

Wiesner, J. (1996): *Parmenides. Der Beginn der Aletheia. Untersuchungen zu B2-B3-B6.* Berlin/New York: de Gruyter.

Wilamowitz-Möllendorf, U. von (1899): "Lesefrüchte." *Hermes* 34, 203-6 [repr. in *Kleine Schriften*, vol. 4, Berlin 1962, 45-8].

Woodbury, L. (1958): "Parmenides on Names." *Harvard Studies in Classical Philology* 63, 145-60.

Zeller, E. (²1856 / ³1869 / ⁶1919): *Die Philosophie der Griechen in ihrer geschichtlichen Entwicklung*, Erster Teil.

NAME INDEX

INDEX OF TOPICS